A collection of stories, poer
nothing, but felt everything.

5AM THOUGHTS:

Stories of a 20-Something

Part 1 & Part 2

Noyah Nailah King

To my Grandmother:
to finish the journal you once started for me. may you continue to
write to me even when you depart this earth, and I will always share
your wisdom with everyone I know.

& To Josh:
this journal missed you by just a few days, but God said you had
more important places to be. you visited me in my dream once, and
reassured me of everything I needed to know. thank you for allowing
me to know you, even if it was just for a little while.

Rubber Ducky Dracula

To write this book at times intimidated me.
I had so much to say & yet I was so nervous to write it all down.
I found myself afraid of my truth.
My life's experiences are what made me.

I have played a crucial role in becoming who I am today.
The unrequited love can't take all of the credit,
and neither can the times where I lacked enough energy to get out of
bed.

To see the life that I am living and witness it all being written on
these pages
is not an easy thing to read,
or comprehend.

~

I try writing when the sun is out, but my paper ends up empty.
My mind races at night with 'what ifs' & endless possibilities.

5am thoughts helped me cope.
It helped me accept the things I cannot change,
and come to terms with what currently is.
The words written on these pages are words of vulnerability & truth.
At 5am I cannot sleep.
I can write.
I can feel.
At 5am, I can really dream.

What are your thoughts at 5am?
Do you wish to be asleep?
I don't.

I appreciate 5am for welcoming me with its' open arms.
In a world where I can create, I enter 5am with an open mind.

5am thoughts free the soul, free the mind, and free my spirit.
Enjoy.

Stories, Poems, & Journals:

Part 1

my mind is all over the place, and so is this book.

"Thrive"

I grabbed my suitcase and began to swiftly pack my things. I was in tears. I felt my eyes swelling up and I couldn't process everything to realize I didn't even grab the most important thing: **underwear**. Where am I going without panties? Clearly I wanna be dirty? I'm already a self-righteous selfish bitch who only thinks of herself and no one else. What will wearing dirty drawls really do to me? Nothing. She doesn't understand. No one gets it. No matter how many times I tell them over and over and over again its like I'm talking to a brick wall. I can tweet about it and make subliminal Facebook posts, which aren't condescending or rude, they're just factual. But still, nobody gets it. All it comes back to is: I'm 16 years old and I know nothing. I know nothing about life, or money, or love. Now the life and money part I get but the love, I mean, come on! I know as much as I'm gonna know and all I know is that I love him. So if she can't accept that then I don't need to be here.

"Where do you think you're going?" Theresa says with this attitude that makes you want to jump out a window.

Ok one second: my mothers name is Theresa, but right now I'm pissed off so instead of calling her 'mom' we're on a first-name basis.

"I don't know just yet, but I'm si.."

Bam.

I was hit. It felt like I was shot in the chest with a 9mm and I'm quickly trying to run to the light. All I can think of is Grey's Anatomy and I hear Dr. Bailey say, "push one of Epi!" It came outta nowhere, too. I felt like the Nick Young meme all over social media. Actually, I *was* the Nick Young meme.

I wanted to ask what the hell was she thinking, but here goes those contractions again. My throat hurts. I can't breathe. I can't speak.

One more second: I get like this when I want to say something but my emotions are taking over. I'm currently trying to register this blow to the head I just encountered by asking myself questions like I'm being interrogated by the police. Is this child abuse? Do I need to call the cops? But if I do that Theresa will have the "yeah i did it" look on her face and imma get my ass beat again so I might as well be silent.

Back to the story.

My mom is crazy. After she borderline made me an orphan, it's like she felt immediate remorse. She starts speaking softer and trying to be more understanding. Now the Nick Young meme is in full effect!

I just want to love and be loved. Why is that so hard? It's already hard enough being young and in love at this age. But then to add the person who you want to ask all these questions you have about it; doubt the love you only knew how to give, sucks.

"I know. I'm young. And I'm in high school. And I have no job, but seriously those factors are honestly played out. What do those honestly have to do with loving someone? I know you don't get it, and I don't expect you to, but can you at least try?"

She gives me the look that I've been begging to see and the contractions stopped.

"Ok", she said.

It wasn't everything I wanted to hear, but it was better than an argumentative rebuttal so I'll take it for now.

She left my room and I looked at my suitcase full of clothes and no underwear and decided to take a nap. After you let out a good cry its always best to take a nap. You wake up feeling better.

"To My Mother"

One day you will leave this Earth
and I am trying to not only mentally
prepare myself for that, but physically as well.

I have to believe, understand, and remind myself
that even though you are not here,
that we will see each other in another lifetime.

I know you're thinking,
"Why on earth are you thinking about this right now?"
But every day I inactively, and sometimes actively think about this.
It is always in the back of my head.

One day you are not going to be here
and I will have to figure out how to survive
without you as my fallback plan.

All of my life I have depended on you to save me;
from what I could not fight on my own, even if it was from myself.

One day you will leave this earth,
so will dad,
and so will my siblings
and I will have to miss them, too.

Everybody loses somebody,
and that should make me feel better,
but it just makes me realize
that when the people closest to me lose someone,
that I will have to be there to help them move forward from that, too.

You are the woman who birthed me,
who fills out my paperwork when I'm lazy,
who taught me every lesson I know to this day.

I sit and think about where I want to go in life
and I can only hope that you will be there
to watch me accomplish everything I've set out to do.

But I have to receive,
understand,
and acknowledge that life doesn't always work out the way we want
it to.

I am writing this in remembrance of you
and you are still here.

But I am preparing myself for the day you no longer will be.
I hope that day is no where near,
but, I know how life can be.

The way life works you would think we would live everyday
playing it safe and close to home.
But that lifestyle is not for me.

I want you to know that this isn't a sad poem
& it is not to make you feel bad or incomplete.

I'm doing this so that when that day does come,
it doesn't hit me so hard to the point that I can't get back up
& stand firmly on my feet.

Thank you mom & dad, for everything.

Journal:

Write a short note to your mother telling her all you wish you could,
would, or should have. Write, release it, and then go do it.

_____

_____

_____

_____

"Pieces"

Pieces of me.
I kept giving away pieces of me.
A kiss. A touch. A stroke.
Emotions weren't even the half of it.
I kept wondering why I couldn't recognize myself more and more each time I looked in the mirror. My eyes were a little bit lower, my cheeks were a little bit harder, and my smile frowned more than ever. It was the pieces of me that I was giving away so freely that I was trying to figure out how to get back. I kept trying to love fully when I wasn't loved wholly.
But in pieces.
Dedicating my mind, my body, my soul, to someone who was giving me
pieces,
of them.
What am I to you?
What was I to you?
I don't want to be cuddled and held by a man I have no intentions of making mine. Am I your temporary passion? Am I your temporary fix? I am not the drug you seek to cultivate your itch. I am not your heroin. You cannot shoot me up & then when you come down from the high you're "clean".
Clean of what? Of me?
Didn't you want me here?
Didn't you want to be here?
He stays the night and after the deed is done he wakes up close to 7am and begins to dress himself, if he even stays. What about breakfast? What about that revolutionary pillow talk?
Why do I deserve you?
Why do you think I deserve you?
What can you do for me that I cannot do for myself?
I can please myself.
I can feed myself.
But what about love?
Can I love myself?
Can I love myself without you?
Without you showing me the ropes?
Is a man necessary to show self-love?

Have I ever really loved myself? By myself? And for myself?
Being a wife to a man who wasn't even your boyfriend.
There was no validity
"But what do we need the title for if everything is good the way it is?"
But do you really need sex from me if you can cum by yourself?
You gave, he took. You signed a contract when you didn't read the fine print.
The pieces have dwindled and now I am trying to re-do the puzzle.
But the pieces are scattered all around.
Each man has a piece of me. They have taken a certain part of me that I am honestly not sure if I want back.
I want a new.
I want him to have a brand new me.
No one deserves me more than me.
To love me. To hold me. To have all of me.
No more pieces.
Whole.

Journal:

Immature love seems to run rapid in your 20-somethings. Are you in a relationship? Or in a habit? Identify the type of love you think you deserve and don't accept anything less than that.

I deserve a type of love that is...

*Ex: Freeing*_____

_____

_____

_____

_____

_____

_____

_____

_____

_____

_____

_____

What I learned.

Another two weeks went by full of inconsistencies and broken
promises and I became exhausted. I think back now and ask myself
why do I give more to people when I receive less than half of them?

For someone who has shown me nothing but
inconsistency,
I kept giving them the benefit of the doubt and being disappointed
when I was let down.

 A lot of my headaches and frustrations could have been avoided if I
had used the word
"no"
more often.
I wasn't in love with him or his actions I was merely in love with his words.

The sweet nothings he spoke were
convenient to me,
too.

At the time I needed what was said because it sounded
good,
even though I had nothing to back up the words that I was being
spewed.

*Let this be a **lesson** to you reading this that sometimes people come into
your life for a season.*

It is not meant for them to stay.
And the more you make them stay the more frustrated you will
become.

He overstayed his welcome plenty of times and it was up to me to
show him the door. Except for when he kept trying to leave, he
would eventually come back and I let him in with no questions asked.

So a lot of what happened to me and between us happened because I
allowed it.

Learn to say "no" and mean it.
Learn that just because they come back, it doesn't mean they were meant to stay.
Learn that is ok for them to go, or for you to go, too.

Save yourself the time and heartache of trying to make someone stay who doesn't deserve to stay. Instead of giving all of you all the time, learn to give yourself half until they prove they deserve the whole thing.

You are worth more than half-ass love.

Release your energy. Especially the negative. What he did before does not make you who you are now. When was the last time you gave a piece of yourself and then made yourself whole?

_____

_____

_____

_____

_____

_____

_____

_____

_____

_____

_____

Sign or Initial

Whole

A Short Story:

The convenience of me wasn't my decision. No matter what I did or how hard I tried that seemed to always be the end point. All of the things you claimed to feel for me you only felt when it was convenient for you. Why do I get the short end of your stick? When you're not even giving me the best dick? The only thing that matched was the inconsistencies of your words and actions. Who am I to really blame? You? Or myself?

2 weeks. I fell head over heels in love with you in two weeks. And not one ounce of physical contact was needed. It was short and simple at first. The typical "get to know you" questions. I think he asked me everything but my favorite color honestly. Everything else seemed more important to him than the basics. I'm not really sure if that's a good or a bad thing.

I was there when things were going good at first. The "Hey Beauty" daily morning messages were the first thing I woke up to and I didn't want it to change so soon. But that wasn't up to me, either. We started to bond over mutual shows we both agreed were entertaining and sort of life changing, even tried to make one another watch the ones we tended to stray away from.

"So what do you like to do for fun?"

This question always freaks me out. The conversation quickly turns from a fun and joyful conversation to a job interview. Am I interviewing to be your wife, or your girl for the night? I was unaware of his intentions and didn't want to think about it too much so I answered, but I proceeded with caution.

"Well I like to shop of course, drink wine, and go to happy hours. I also love to do outdoorsy type of stuff like rock climbing, kayaking, and archery. I was a Girl Scout counselor a few years back so it's like kind of second nature to me. And I also like taking naps."

Question, when you first meet a guy and you guys are "talking" or whatever you call it, do you feel as if you are trying to sell yourself? You're trying to list all of your good qualities that make you seem "wife" material so you don't scare him away so easily. I'm not really sure if that's a good or a bad thing, either.

But he answered with his calculated response of uplifting how "different" from other females I was and his elevator speech and finally that part was over. I couldn't tell if he was getting to know me to undress my mind, or undress me.

I knew he was hurt from a previous injury so I sent him a "good luck" text in the morning and per my friends that was against "The Rules". You know, the rules of how to get a man, and how to keep a man. Clearly I was pressed.

Nightly FaceTime calls began to pick up and conversations got deeper, but very sexual. Sex was my type of thing though. It wasn't one of the first things I'd tell someone of course. But he matched my sex drive. Pictures were everything. Maybe not the smartest thing. But it was just enough to keep the imagination flowing.

Things started to get more intense and in the back of my mind I kept telling myself we should slow down, but I also was thinking if we were both having fun and apparently on the same page, why would I stop it? I've dealt with so many different guys in the past and I didn't want him to end up like another unwritten story. I couldn't tell if I being insecure or just plain uptight so I didn't say anything but continued to go with the flow.

Who knew that going with the flow would leave you heartbroken?

He was further in distance than a place I could reach at the time, but I was so borderline in love I even began to look up flights and racking up points on my credit card. But I have always felt as if distance is just temporary.

Things started to move more quickly as some of his family began to follow me on social media and he even sent me a screenshot of a picture, of me, that he sent his mother. I was so excited by the fact that there was a man who was so invested in me and showing me to the people he loved the most, I mean who wouldn't love that?

16

The first problem we shared was the fact that he noticed I had a lot of male friends, and I couldn't help that. The boyfriend of mine who died a few years back left an army of best friends who then became my best friends, including a few others too. I didn't feel like that was something I needed to apologize for or ever compromise, but I did feel the need to explain it to him in a little more detail so that he could fully understand. The conversation went fine and I thought he understood their place in my life, but what I hadn't realized was it left open more questions than it had answers.

I was relieved that that topic was discussed and we began to talk about us and our future more. We began to plan summer beach trips and even a potential trip to visit his parents which had me more than excited. Once he began to express more of the conversations he had with his mom about me I thought I'd share to my mom about him, too. I was a little hesitant, but I figured since he's doing the same why not do it. I spilled the beans to my mom, but I spared her with very little details as I wasn't exactly convinced this was someone who needed be introduced just yet. I was hopeful and optimistic, but not convinced. Those are two very different things.

Mind you there was no physical contact happening between either of us other than our FaceTime calls and random sexting, but the question of birth control was brought up and he asked was I on it. "No", I replied, with the intent to let him know that if need be, I would make the switch. I had stayed away from birth control for 21 years because of the myths and fears that one day when I do decide that I want to have baby with the love of my life, I wouldn't be able to. So up and until now I relied on safe sex, some times, and luck. But he made it very clear to me after sending him pictures that I needed to be on birth control, or we would be having kids. Because he had no intentions of practicing the "pull out" method. How irresponsible when you think about it. But when someone that you borderline love tells you that he would put babies in you you start to imagine the idea, even when you have no means to carry a child.

He started to show little signs of jealousy and what girl doesn't like a little jealousy from her man? He wasn't "my man", but he was pretty damn close. If someone commented something a little extra on my Instagram pic or sent me an unsolicited tweet, he'd ask questions. Sometimes they were intense questions, others it was just a simple "who is he?" But even though I sensed a little insecurity, I soaked it all up. Because we, as women, love it when a man is so concerned with who is concerned about us. The feeling of being yours is almost as great as the feeling of being our own.

He was out in the world chasing his dreams and then life happened. You know when you're on the ride of life and everything is going well, and then you feel like every 6 months something shitty happens to you to remind you that maybe you're not as cool as you think you are? Well that happened to him. I tried to listen and be supportive, even when it made me uncomfortable. But I put my concerns to the side and tried to be a "wifey". **Mistake #1.**

Never be a wife to someone who is not your husband.

Write that down.

I thought I knew that already, though. But it seemed easier to say out loud than to do to someone who was playing the husband role.

A few days passed and our conversations quickly became shorter. At first, nothing had changed, but then one day I felt something in my gut and overlooked it because I didn't want to seem like a crazy bitch. *But make a note to yourself that when you feel something in your gut, it's there for a reason.* I sometimes think back and ask myself that if I hadn't ignored my intuition telling me I was right, would I have ended up in such mess? Maybe everything could've been avoided if I listened to myself and not the potential of a man that wasn't really telling me anything.

Monday came and this is the first day since we started communicating that we hadn't spoken. I was at work and was busy with work stuff so I didn't have to think and dwell on it all day, but it was still in the back of my head. I checked my phone every 5 minutes and received no text. If I wasn't pressed before I was definitely pressed now. It's funny now that I think about it; that a mans words and not even his presence can have me caught up like this (refer to Love is Blind). Checking my dry-ass phone to make sure I didn't miss anything. It was pathetic. But I finally got something.

"I think we should slow down".
My heart sunk. But the first thing that went through my head was, "I knew it".

We had just had a conversation two nights before and it was definitely off. I expressed to him that instead of going ghost, I'd rather him just talk to me about it so we could work it out. Because when you disappear for whatever reason, I think that it could be about me. Even though I could be 100% wrong, I wouldn't know unless you told me. Plus, I think it's just common fucking curtesy.

He told me he understood but I wasn't exactly confident in his response, but I also didn't want to be annoying. I began to notice that when I expressed my concern or something that was important to me, he didn't take it seriously. But when he wanted to talk about something that was important to him, he would expect me to devote my undivided attention. **Mistake #2.**

"Okay", was all I responded to his text. I mean, I didn't know what else to say. I can't argue with you about how you feel, but I also can't deny how pissed I was.

"I'm not going anywhere, I just want us to slow down a little bit", he said next.

In between the few hours of receiving that text and sending mine I had cooled down and had a little bit of time to think. This was not the first time I had been pursued and received a text like this, which is where 95% of my frustration came from. In my mind I'm like, if you've said all of these sweet words and said you were gonna do all of these awesome things, including me, why would you want to slow down? But then it hit me that sweet words and sweet nothings are exactly the same.

In my time of reflection I also started to think about all that had happened to lead up to this point, what exactly did I do to get here, and how could I have prevented it? The more and more I thought the big question finally popped up in my head, so I asked it:

"Did you feel this way before or after you realized your life wasn't going the way you planned it to be?"

The answer to that question really made a difference to me in how I was going to go about this conversation. Whether I was going to be

super pissed, or a little pissed with more understanding. Either way I was pissed and I just wanted answers.
"*Honestly*, after", he said.

My heart sunk.

Immediately things started adding up. When things were going good for him, then I was good for him. But now he has to rethink some life plans, and nothing serious, but now he has to rethink what he's going to do next, I'm not needed. And I know "slow it down" doesn't mean "we're over", but in my ears it did. Because he made me feel convenient. Here I am, making myself feel uncomfortable to support you, so that I can lift you up and you leave me when you get to the top. Except, you didn't even get there yet. You flaked out when life threw you a hard ball. So when things are going good, it's good. But when things get a little bit rocky, you run, and that's not fair to me.

I didn't say anything at the time because I wanted to wait it out and remember, not be a crazy bitch. I was taking notes every step of the way. Now that he showed me how he responds when life gets tricky, I knew I couldn't really depend on him.
"I felt I was being pressured", was his next statement.

And then the anger came.

When did I ever make you feel pressured? Everything we had ever said or did was because you led the way. I didn't pursue you, I didn't chase you, you led and I followed. And maybe that was the problem. I shouldn't have done that from the beginning. Yes, maybe I pressured you to come and visit me, but you kept giving the notion that thats what you were planning to do so I don't see where the miscommunication was.

I apologized, when maybe I shouldn't really have.

He took a trip to his home town to clear his head and we really didn't talk that much. I guess we both needed the time to get our heads together so I took the opportunity to get myself together as well.

While he was visiting his family he made comments to me like "I miss talking to you", and my rebuttal was always "we are where we are now, because of you". He hated hearing that, but I didn't care because he couldn't take responsibility for his actions.

About a week passed on and our conversation got better, but there was another conversation about me having male friends. I thought I had expressed in our previous conversation that I was never going to compromise my friendships for a man that has yet to commit to me, and even when a man does. Mind you me and my guy friends weren't even up each others ass they are just my platonic friends. But he kept telling me me I was "too friendly". We never even touched in the video so I don't understand how friendly you can be. And he still felt that way even when I expressed the relationship of how close me and my guy friends were. But that didn't matter to him.

That conversation ended with him telling me that he felt as if we would be better off as friends because he doesn't want me to change myself, and he cant ask me not to be friends with certain people. Which that he was correct about so I let him go. I figured any man who is not secure within himself and him and I, we do not need to be together.

He texted me later that night around 3am and sending me a, "sorry I was trippin', can I call you in the morning so we could talk." **Mistake #3.**

I should have left him alone right then and there, honestly. I had asked my brother for some advice, and he told me this:

"No man is ever really comfortable with his girl having a lot of guy friends, so I see where he's coming from. But for the girl, if you really want to be with her, you wouldn't let that effect your relationship. So if he really wanted to be with you, he would make an effort to get to know your guy friends, and he wouldn't let that come in between you."

Why we continued communicating after this I'm not even sure.

I had all of these red flags and I made very little effort to hang up this 'situationship'. We still had no physical contact so I don't really even know what was going on, but I knew it wasn't worth the stress and headache, so I started to put less and less effort into it.

"I am learning to love the sound of my feet walking away from things that are no longer meant for me."-unknown

Journal:

I was never good at letting people go, even when their time in my life had come to an end. There were times where I was not ready for them to leave my life & to prepare myself, I began to accept things for what they were and not what I envisioned they should be.

How do you let people go? Even when you want them to stay, what do you say to someone you know is supposed to walk away?

_____

_____

_____

_____

_____

_____

_____

_____

_____

_____

_____

_____

Break

Lust vs Worth

I had sex with him. That guy I was talking about. And it left me more confused than I was before. I had accepted my consequences beforehand, though. I was aware that if things went left between us I would be ok. I knew what I was doing because I shaved. I said to myself, "If he doesn't talk to me after this, I'll be okay with it". I mean, I wasn't fully okay with it but I understood the repercussions of my decision if they happened to go that way. But my biggest question that I failed to answer until after the fact, was that if he was acting the way he did before I had sex with him, now that he has the only thing he could use over my head. What would make him change? And that is when I realized my lust for him was bigger than my worth. Even though that's not entirely true, it was in the moment. I knew about his inconsistencies and his failure to appear when I needed him most, except I overlooked it. And sitting here now trying to depend on my acceptance, is much harder than I thought.

I am not whole yet.

"Dear Black Girl, stop carrying the guilt from the sins of the men who have wronged you."

\- @reeciology

A Lesson.

Sometimes I get so carried away that I can't find myself anymore. I don't know how I become it or how I get away from it, but there I am, lost. I don't know why I expect so much from people either. It's such a bad habit and I can't seem to break it.

Here's what happens:

I meet a guy.
We text.
We hang out.
Go on a date.
I convince myself that sleeping with him now or later wont make a difference on if he decides to leave me or not, because if that was his intention he was gonna do it regardless.
I then, sleep with him.
We text some more.
Hang out some more.
Sleep together some more.
Then I begin to ask questions.
(mind you all of this is happening in a time span of 2 weeks)
"what are we?"
"where's this going?"
not realizing that this begins to scare them away
I then begin to attempt to protect my heart when I gave up that right a long time ago in dealing with him.
I also began to expect certain things as if we are in a relationship and we are not, which then causes us to end.

And it's a cycle. It repeats like clock work. And I'm exhausted. How do I break this cycle? How do I protect my heart from the beginning instead of waiting until it's too late? Why have I lowered my standards and worth so that it's easier for others to reach it?

A Summer's Lesson

This whole summer I didn't realize it, but I had lost my self-worth. It took me three and a half months to come to terms with myself, and no one else. I kept looking to other people for confirmation and confidence, in the decisions that I would ultimately have to make myself. I would know the right thing to do, but I would let my temporary feelings cloud my judgment. The things and people I would allow into my life were a reflection of how I felt about myself. I would accept being lied to and led on thinking that I deserved this. I knew I didn't, but I had somehow convinced myself that if I didn't put up with it, I didn't deserve the end result: happiness. It has taken me three and half months to answer myself. I've been asking the same questions, "why do I keep going through this?" and "why do I keep running into people like this?". The answer is because I let it. I'm not ever going to take responsibility for the actions of others by no means, because they are responsible for themselves and their intentions. But what I can take is responsibility for is my availability. *Everyone isn't allowed to know me.* It is my responsibility to be conscious and aware. Once I was aware of what was going on around me, and I chose to either ignore it, or try to change it, the outcome was my fault. So in this last summer month, I have learned that I need to re-learn how to love myself. I love myself, and I respect myself, because that's what I was taught to do growing up. But it took me being put in situations where people did not love and respect me, to learn how much I have devalued myself by realizing what I have allowed. I do not wish bad on anyone, by any means, I just wish more love and happiness to myself.

"People often look for advice on things they already know to reaffirm the decision they don't necessarily want to make." -
@wordsncurves

I wonder why we whine and cry when God removes people who are no longer good for us out of our lives. It never made sense to me how I get so upset when a person who had terrible intentions and a temporary placement decides to walk away from my life. Maybe it was because of the comfortability? I'm not exactly sure. I need to become confident in who is here, and who is not.

I'm hurting right now, and I can't wait until I've let it go. I figure that writing it down would be better. Things could be worse, of course. But that doesn't take away the pain of whats happening right now. I'm tired of falling in love with men who aren't ready. I'm always a few steps ahead of them. Society tells us that we as women are supposed to prepare a man who isn't ready to love us, love us. That we are supposed to let him make his mistakes and we're supposed to stick by him, and when we don't it's frowned upon. Why is that? What about me making mistakes, and what if I'm "not ready"? Would a man stick by me? Usually when we're told that we have to stick by a man through thick & thin it involves us being shitted on and disrespected, but thats all apart of the process right? What process is that and where was that written? The only process of love that I know is the one that I read in the bible. A man seeks out a woman. He courts her, learns her, overwhelms her with love and support. He looks at her as if she was him and he was her. I am not a midnight adventure. I am not someone who you can take a break from and come and find when you're ready. I keep finding myself in situations with boys who will tell me that I'm perfect for them 5 years from now. Well what about now? I even had a boy tell me that in the meantime while he was "getting himself together" that I should focus on me, and build up my brand so that when he's ready we can just 'pick up where we left off'. I dropped him right then and there. I will focus on me because thats what I want to do. Not because thats what you told me to do.

Pledge of Allegiance

It sucks. Being molded by situationships. I'm naturally a planner so 'going with the flow' has always given me anxiety. Just recently I realized that I don't know my worth. And that's not entirely true because I do know my worth, I just haven't been acting like I do. It was hard for me to listen to someone tell me this because I honestly thought I had it all together, but then it hit me that I didn't.

Unfortunately, this generation loves the "talking" stage. Basically it's the process of dating someone, but not being committed to them. But it's very ambiguous and mysterious and only works out for you if you're not emotionally invested. I've learned that this generation is so afraid to emotionally commit. They're afraid to love, but they want to be loved. So they'll put their foot halfway in the door when getting to know someone, while the other person is usually not holding back, which causes confusion and ultimately the process starting over with someone new. And that's why I'm so exhausted. The process keeps starting over with the same old situation and the same old outcome that I can't trust fully nor love fully. And that's unfortunate for me because when the man that really deserves to know me does come along, I'm going to struggle giving myself to him because I've been giving myself to all these other people who had no interest in investing in me.

Your worth is something that is to be defined by you and you only. No one else can tell you what you're worth, and just because of someone's inability to see your worth, doesn't mean you're not worthy. I kept dealing with people who didn't see my worth and I questioned myself is it because I didn't make them see? But are you supposed to make people see your worth? Are you supposed to convince them everything that you bring to the table? I'm not exactly sure about that, but I do think you can help them out a little bit. I had been dealing with so many guys and the outcome was always the same. I would find myself courting them and it not being reciprocated. I would ask all of the questions to get to know them deeper and on a more intimate level, but I was never asked any. I found myself getting frustrated at always being in the same predicament so something had to give. I needed to take a step back and realize my worth.

I am worthy because I say that I am worthy. I am a woman who has made more mistakes than I can count on my fingers, but that does not define me. I keep giving myself to men who only want me until the morning and I even find myself sad when they leave. I wasn't like this until recently and I'm trying to figure out where I went wrong. Is my inability to be patient so misconstrued that I'll settle for anything and anybody? Why am I like this? Why do I keep putting myself through this?

I think I've figured it out and then the same thing happens and I find myself back at square one. It's like I take 3 steps forward but 5 steps back.

But today I make a pledge to myself. Because I know my worth, and I know the type of woman I am and what I deserve I will not settle for anything less than that. Because I'm aware of what I bring to the table and the potential that I have. I won't settle for anything less than that either.

I wonder why we, as women, fall in love with potential more than what we see right in front of us. I've fallen in love with so much potential that I didn't even recognize who I was directly looking at. I knew what he could be 5 years from now so in the meantime I have to put up with the inconsistency, the lying, and the constant belittling to get him to where he needs to be. I'll tell myself to wait for him to grow up, to wait for him to man up, but why won't I do the same? And we mess up when we get a man who see's the potential, but they don't want to reach that potential themselves. Because potential is just that, it's potential. Nothing more, nothing less.

You are not entitled to a mans potential. *What he could be vs what he would rather be are two different things.* His potential was far more greater than he ever was and I loved it.

Break

No one likes feeling used. No matter the circumstance or situation it's just not an ideal feeling.
What's worse about it is when you're being used by someone who you would never do that to.
You find yourself in an empty headspace.
Trying to figure out where you went wrong and how you could've avoided feeling this shitty.
Most of the time though it's really not you, it's them and their cruel intentions.
Of course there were things you could've done to protect yourself, but you chose to be vulnerable and let your guard down because you trusted so easily.
So you blame and beat yourself up and claim that you're gonna build this emotional wall up so you'll never have to deal with it again.
But, life. Life puts us through situations to make us learn something. If you listen closely you'll hear what life is trying to teach you.
A lot of times potential relationships get screwed up because of a lack of communication. Being vocal changes the dynamic of everything.
People being confident in their intentions and reasonings help build successful friendships and relationships.
A lot of the time what I found myself coming across were people who would hide their true intentions and put on a facade for an end goal.
When you find out you've been led on and basically hunted like a wild animal you become angry and almost unapologetically revengeful.
Do not let this happen to you.
It is not your fault what is done to you, but it is when you begin to allow it.
I had been told by multiple sources that his intentions were not pure, but I decided to find out for myself and continue putting up with inconsistency and excuses for the lack there of.
When I finally got him right where I wanted him just to get the somewhat truth out of him,
I began to use my words and my fake potential actions as bait.
Once a man is horny he will say anything and you will learn to use this to your advantage.
The conversation grew thicker and when I received the "come thru" text I became nauseous.

I had no intentions of coming through anywhere and yet however I had to say just what I needed to say to get him to come clean.
I threw out more bait by bringing up the fact I couldn't trust his word and even got him to ask how was he going to make it up to me. That's when I knew, I had him.
This is when I needed to pay close attention to what I was saying because this could make or break everything.
Hopefully he didn't see my intentions, & from the looks of it he didn't.
I finally revealed my Queen card like we were playing a game of solitaire and I had all the evidence that led up to King lined up right behind it.
I said, "We couldn't even have sex because I'm on my period."
This was true by the way, I just knew if I said it he'd either be like "that doesn't matter" or "yea no reason for you actually coming".
Because if he really cared about me and didn't need my body for just sex, that wouldn't have even been an issue.
Except the response was, "you can come over if you find a way to relieve my stress".
That hit hard.
I was expecting for him to say something fucked up but not *that* fucked up lmao.
I had never felt so disrespected in my life.
I asked myself was this really happening to me and how did I get to this point to allow him to even feel comfortable to say those words to me?
I thought I had proven myself to be a woman of her word.
A woman who accepted not only words, but actions as its evidence and a woman who wouldn't tolerate disrespect from anybody.
But I guess he figured since I had been tolerating disrespect for weeks that him saying that would be no problem. And he was right.
He wasn't right for doing it, but because I had allowed him to do everything else, he felt that it was okay.
I thanked him to myself for finally showing his intentions, but then it hit me that he had been showing his true intentions all along.
Between the arguments for inconsistency and God knows what else, all the red flags were there and I chose to ignore them.
When he said those words I was so disappointed in myself and what I allowed I even almost wanted to cry.
I knew beforehand the outcome and yet I just wanted to see it for myself so I couldn't complain because this is what I asked for.

Since this generation loves casual sex so much, if he would've been vocal about that from the beginning then I probably would've entertained it, and knowing that hurt me too.
I was pissed because he would rather use me and my body like a prized possession than to be confident in his intentions and my decision to either accept or deny them.
Men get so scared that if they tell a woman that he just wants to have sex with her that she might not want to so she'll decide not to entertain it.
Most of the time that is true, but some times it isn't.
But what pissed me off the most was that I wasn't even given a choice. It was decided for me what was my value to him.
It was decided for me that that was my worth.

Even when I asked him was this what we have became he denied it, and yet his actions showed otherwise. Find someone who wants the same things as you and flourish. Don't lie and beat around the bush to get what you want out of people, that's fucked up. Find someone who wants what you want and go from there. Give them the option to decide and if they decide that's not what they want then move on. There are plenty more fish in the sea. Why do you have to deprive this one of water?

A THANK YOU LETTER

August 10, 20-something

Dear you,

I want to genuinely thank you for all that
you have done in these few short weeks of
knowing you. It took meeting you for me to
understand my worth. In the beginning, I was so
lost. It was like I valued being vulnerable
more than I valued my own body. I embraced your
potential instead of being a conscious witness
to your truth. **You were needed in order for me
to grow.** Without you, I don't know if I
would've learned the lesson God has been trying
to teach me for so long now.

My body is a temple, and it took me giving
it to you and you using it to your advantage
for me to finally realize that. I gave and you
took, as if you were entitled, and you were
not. I do not want you to feel as if I am being
condescending in this letter because that is
not my intention. I want you to truly and
honestly grasp that I am so very thankful for
you and the amount of emotional hell you put me
through. It was sickening, but it was
necessary. I pray you find happiness in the
place that you lost it.

Sincerely,
A 20-Something

A THANK YOU LETTER

In the moments where you beat yourself up about something
you cannot change, instead create a frequent reminder to
forgive & remind yourself that everything is going to be ok.

_____, 20-something

Dear you,

_____
_____
_____
_____
_____
_____

_____
_____
_____
_____
_____
_____

Sincerely,
A *20-Something*

"Dear Black Girl, you are not responsible for the burden of anyone else's emotions but your own, so don't silence your truth to protect his lies." - @reeciology

When we met the timing was detrimental,
to both you and I.
I was trying to fall out of love,
and not be so blind.
The next chapter was beginning,
two directions is where we went.
You North and I South,
I questioned would we ever meet again.
Unimportant.

Time flew by and the growth had developed.
I saw you and I squinted because I just couldn't tell if.
I was still falling out and you were reeling me in,
I was more prone to slip up and commit an accident.
No accident this was, it was self made.
Affiliating myself with you but you began to barricade.
I questioned, you answered. Nothing gets solved.
The friendship was more important,
or was it just flawed?
Sick.

I suppressed them until my stomach hurt,
making me feel nauseous.
'For the greater good' I thought,
I dropped a feeling and instead I caught it.
I made excuses and time began to fade,
I wonder what would have happened,
if you actually loved me enough to change.
Life.

Unrequited Love/Break

I felt like I was owed an award, ya know?
Like a trophy or medal.
I was able to overlook my feelings for him and maintain a friendship
without having to choose between one or the other.
It was years ago when I started to look at him differently.
Even when we were intimate, I didn't entertain the thought of
anything more than a friendship.
My boyfriend had just died and I was looking for a way out and I
figured he was it.
It wasn't until after that I realized he was much more than that, to
me at least.
Our friendship grew over time through sporadic communication and
frequent visits.
We passed different tests over the years that made our friendship
strong enough
to withstand almost anything.
But I didn't think it would be this.
I once asked him how he felt about me and he told me,
"I have those feelings for you some times,
but not all the time,
and that means we should just keep our friendship where it is,
because I don't want to hurt you."
You know what I've always wondered?
When someone turns you down or breaks your heart
you have to commend them for not doing it in a mean way.
I felt like I was suppressing my feelings to account for the lack of his.
I haven't made the love that I feel for him too important
because our friendship is more important than any other romantic
relationship,
or lack thereof, we've ever had.
But there I was, loving him anyway.
The feeling wasn't going away.
But I had to be the bigger person.
The stronger person.
How was I going to be the stronger person if my feelings were
stronger than his?

"Unrequited love,
to me it's like a one-man cult,
a cyanide in my styrofoam cup,
I could never make him love me."
 - Frank Ocean

The type of bond we shared

was unlike any other.
you were my best friend
more than a significant other.
I cherished our friendship
as it withstood time and hardships.
but life changed for the both of us.
you went down one path and i went the other.
i tried so hard for us to conjoin paths and walk with each other.
you had your way of doing things
as i had mine.
but the one thing i never questioned
was the love i felt inside.
you did something for me that i can never forget.
something that i don't know if without you i would ever have had the
chance to get.
i tried so hard to tell you
not to be so hard on yourself.
you are not God,
you are not perfect,
so stop comparing yourself.
you wanted to seek him,
and i wasn't there yet.
i was on the path to get there
except i was moving a little slower.
i did not fault you for not waiting on me.
but i did not expect you to leave me behind.
as a Christian,
i was taught that you were supposed to be a vessel.
you selfishly loved God and felt that if i did not
practice my love for him in the same way you did
then my love was false.
that to me, was not of God.

this is for the both of you.

Notes:

Truth:

You will meet many different people in your life and some of them
you will not have a choice but to love them. I've never been one to
boast about not having many real friends because I've always
surrounded myself with nothing but the realist. But in a matter of a
year, I have lost two very important people to me, and neither one of
them is dead. That hurts.

The Art of Forgiving Yourself

"To forgive is to set a prisoner free and discover that that prisoner was you." - unknown

When I was first introduced to love I met a young boy who shared with me everything he knew. I made tributes about our love. It was the only love I had ever known at the time. This isn't a story about the love I fell in and eventually, fell out of. This is the happily ever after. I spent so many years asking God do I even get a "happily ever after". I travelled the world looking for answers and the only thing I ended up finding was myself. At 22 years old I have experienced more heartbreak in a lifetime than most average-aged adults. That's not something that I usually share with everyone, and it's definitely not something that I usually boast about. But in this instance, it's very important that I include that tiny detail so you can get a better understanding of my life and why I make the decisions I do. Most of the things that have happened to me over the course of my life I wouldn't wish on my worst enemy. But they happened, and for that I am grateful because it made me, me.

Before I go on to share my experience about black love I want to say, "my pro-blackness does not make me anti-white, it just makes me also pro-black", except I feel the same about love as most do about the Black Lives Matter movement and any other movement created by and for the advancement of African-Americans.

The love that I experienced has been extremely black. From the way we catch up on the night before with one person on the toilet and the other brushing their teeth. From the way we grocery shop with a "cut & take" like mindset to stay in our budget of $125. The love that I've met has influenced my life in every way.

I'm 22 years old and I've been in love twice in my lifetime. Fortunately, they were both with men who loved me back. I understand that not everyone has that luxury, so my experience isn't based on a love that is unrequited.

Question:

Have you noticed that a lot of couples thrive in their dysfunction? The high of getting into an argument, saying whatever needs to be said to get it off your chest whether it is disrespectful or hurtful, just to come back together and call your relationship "unbreakable" is a bad habit in itself. So many couples romanticize the break ups and not the healthy factors that actually ensure a long-lasting healthy relationship.

I've found that it is very easy to get ahead of yourselves in relationships. You're in month 6 but in your head you two have been together for 6 years and you're expecting a proposal tomorrow. Some partners find this exciting that you're thinking so far ahead into the future making plans for the both of you, but others find it discouraging.

I've found that in order to forgive you have to let something go. If you find yourself being a prisoner in your own mind, maybe you should let yourself go. **Set yourself free**.

Daddy Issues

My father was a smart man.
He was successful and paid very close attention to his work.
I sometimes asked why I could not receive the same.

I waited.
and waited.
and waited.
But he never showed up.

I was sitting outside on the porch,
with my bags packed and I grabbed a jacket just in case things got chilly.
and I waited.

I was excited to take a trip with just me and my dad.
I wanted more of him.
I *craved* more of him.

Time went on and as I sat there still waiting I realized that he was not coming.

I asked my mom, "why doesn't he like me very much?"
She said daddy was just busy.
I just wanted to him to show up.

At 22 years old I learned a lot more about my dad and I'm unsure if he really wanted me to.

Waiting for people to show up is a waste of time.
It's a waste of yours,
and it is a waste of theirs.

Just because someone doesn't show up doesn't mean they don't want to.

Sometimes they aren't capable of it at the moment.
You forget that sometimes they go through things, too.
And you shouldn't take it personal.

I blamed myself for his lack of commitment to me, his child.

But I've grown up to realize that he was the best person he could be, and that he loved me the best way he knew how.

Years later after his passing I have forgiven him.
I am no longer waiting for you to show up,
But I will always show up for you.

Ever since I met you I smile differently.
I know that hard times won't be as hard because I'll have you
there with me.
You make me believe I can do the impossible,
and you make me feel safe.
When I hug you it feels like home,
and when I kiss you it feels like forever.
I'm in love with everything you are and have yet to be.
I heard you needed this so I figured I'd grab it.
Thank you for being you and loving me the way you do.

forgiven.

God is Greater than our Ups and Downs
5:37AM

The first time I ever experienced jealousy was when my God-sister growing up had a best friend. I was confused because at the time I didn't understand how friendships worked. I thought when you were friends with someone, your friendship was exclusive in all areas, including other friends. They would hang out and of course, be friends, and that threw me in for a loop. As time went on and I created friendships with other people I began realize that it's ok.

I think growing up you begin realize that maintaining friendships with other people is just as important as maintaining a friendship with yourself. As I think back to all of the friendships I've accumulated over the years, I realized how I've personally grown in my friendships. There were times where I was mistreated and there were definitely times that I could have been a better friend myself.

Growing up I went to the same church every Sunday and most of the time I went for my friends and not to actually involve myself in anything church. I was younger so I knew what I was taught and didn't really have a mind of my own in terms of religion or spirituality yet, so it was OK for the time being. There were a group of friends I had grown up with and we were in our teens around this time. We would all hang out with each other after church and have sleepovers or beg our parents to go home with one another after Sunday school ended to continue on our friendship. There were 3 guys and 3 girls outside who I would really associate myself with. 3 guys who were brothers, 1 girl who was any god-sister, one new girl to the church, and a girl I didn't really like deep down but they all associated with her so I was forced to. I had no real idea of friendship so a lot of time there were rumors we'd spread about each other within the group, pass judgment etc. whatever the case may be. As I started growing up my god-sister and I grew apart but I don't personally think that was for a specific reason. I've grown to learn that sometimes friends are still friends even if they don't speak everyday. There was another family at our church of all brothers and they had one older sister as well. Their family was widely known in Greensboro and his dad was like a pastor himself. At least, when I was younger that's what I would think. One of the brothers I became very fond with and even though we didn't speak that often I'd like to think we created our own special relationship. We didn't ever hang out outside of church but we'd speak to each other and he just made me want to know him more. Unfortunately at the age I was, I never did.

Some time went on and a crush developed but I noticed it also did between him and the girl I didn't really like very much. Now if I didn't like her much before I definitely didn't like her much now. I just remember that we created some sort of beef between each other and him and his family eventually left the church and went to a different one. Not because of our beef though, lol.

Throughout our distaste for each other we developed a friendship. Through the years of our friendship, I'm sure there were some instances where I could have been a better friend, and there were some times she could have been too. Our friendship withstood a lot of trials and tribulations in my life which is why I considered her my Person. She was the first person I called when the death of my boyfriend, and then, just a crush, died my senior year of high school. I was there for her throughout her parents almost divorce. Luckily for her, they didn't divorce and I was there throughout that celebration as well. She was someone I considered a first love. Theres a first romantic type of love, and there's also a first platonic. I counted on her for almost everything . To help me see whatever battle I was facing through. Unfortunately somewhere in our friendship over the years, something went wrong. Over the past several months I've been trying to pinpoint exactly at which point it was. I know that when you're hurt you say some hurtful things, but there's some things you just don't say. Throughout our friendships, there were more victories than arguments.

What I've learned with relationships platonic & romantic, they're the same in a lot of ways. Communication, trust, honestly, loyalty, they're all transparent in any type of relationship you form. I couldn't think back to a time where our relationship was really lacking in any of those areas. In terms of communication, it's not unlikely that you and your friend don't communicate every day. Especially when one of you gets a new boyfriend and the other is trying to figure out life for herself. I appreciated her boyfriend because he could love her in a way that I would never know how. And that was ok for me. That didn't mean I didn't love her as my best friend any more or any less. Of course at times I was jealous because I felt like a lot of her time was being taken up, but that's because it was. I think that you as a friend have to balance the time you spend with each other and others. And in the beginning there could have been a better balance and that may have put an initial strain on our relationship

Sometimes, you go through rough patches with your friends. It doesn't make you any less of friends, it just makes you human. I find that happening sometimes in the relationship I have with my significant other. He may be going through something that he's not talking to you about and may be short with his words. It causes you both to develop some type of unintended animosity towards each other and every simple exchange between you two ends up being an argument. I've learned that in the same way that you are encouraged to learn your significant others love language to ensure compatibility, that same energy should be applied when dealing with your platonic friendships as well. Learn the way your friends accept apologies, and how they deal when they are angry with you. Now, I am able to easily recognize when there is a disconnect within my friendships and how to quickly assess the problem. Real friends are hard to come by. So you have to decide within yourself who is worth the fixing of issue of disconnect.

GROWTH

and how it sometimes doesn't just change you, but the people around you.

I've felt the heartbreak about a few different things in my life so far. I was heartbroken when my dog died from a seizure, and my sister and dad found him laying on the floor when they returned home one afternoon. I was heartbroken when I genuinely liked a boy in college, but he liked my body a lot more instead. I was heartbroken when I didn't receive the internship I had applied for my junior year, after I had spent hours of working on the application and hoping they'd accept me. And after all of these heartbreaks nothing ever compared to the heartbreak of losing your best friend.

There have been moments in my life where I've felt the pain of growth and accepted it because it was something that was not only positive, but needed. Throughout these growth periods I changed parts about myself not only by choice, but by circumstance. Whether you want to believe it or not, life and the situations you go through change you. Throughout the changes that I not only witnessed, but the people around me witnessed as well, not everyone could handle and accept it.

I wanted to change. I strived to change and grow into the woman I always saw myself becoming. There were friends who knew me before any of what I encountered in my life and were with me to witness as well. And there were people who became friends after which I went through certain things that shaped me into who I am and was going to be.

Before I entered college, I was always warned about the pain of growth, but never the pain of losing close friends that came with it. As you go through life you will go through certain things that will change your outlook on life, yourself, and the people around you. You may find yourself growing at a more rapid pace than the people you associate yourself with on a day-to-day basis. That doesn't mean you aren't friends and still cant be friends, it just means you're growing faster than they are and that's ok.

I found myself learning more and evolving into this woman who I had never met before. She was outspoken, more confident, and had an entrepreneurial like mindset. I didn't realize that this scared some people away from me. In the midst of my growing I had friends with whom I didn't speak to everyday. I didn't feel like this made us any less of friends, I just figured life had gotten in the way of our frequent communication, but we would check up on each other and I was ok with that. Sometimes our conversations were deep, some were short, and some lasted for hours just talking about nothing.

It takes a lot of communication, trust, honesty, and so much more qualities to keep any type of relationship afloat, but it takes effort from both sides. In the relationship that I have with my significant other we check up on each other every day. Although we have a life and a relationship collectively together we both also have lives separate from each other. And to make sure that we don't ever overlook one another and miss out on each other's outside lives, we have to reconnect with each other on a daily basis and there's nothing wrong with that. Friendships work the same. You're in school, joining a bunch of clubs, making a lot of new friends but none of that should take away from the relationships you've already built. You still have to check up on each other to keep the relationship healthy and sustainable.

In this particular relationship, I had felt like I had done my part. Do I think there were times where I could have been difficult? Of course. Do I think there were times where I wasn't the easiest person to talk to? Absolutely. But in those moments when you're dealing with someone who you consider of value to you, you communicate those issues and you work through them. In this instance, in this very conversation where I had been blind-sided by all of these feelings and oppositions, I realized I was not of value to someone who I valued much more than life itself.

There's some people you meet and you can tell they're going to be in your life forever. You include them in your daydreams, you include them in things like weddings and baby showers, you plan just about everything around their availability because you want them involved. But there are also people you meet and you say to yourself, "hm, I can tell we're going to be associates but I don't ever see us being that close". Or you have people in your life who you put a time limit on how long you're even going to be friends in general because you don't see that much longevity.

I knew life had happened but I didn't think our friendship had to end because of it. I shortly realized that after the going back and forth that I had outgrown you. I didn't necessarily choose or plan to, if I could take you with me I could. But you solidified friends who were on the same path and current level as you. I knew that but it never crossed my mind that our friendship had to stop growing because we started growing in two different paces.

I was heartbroken. For months I was heartbroken about a friendship that lasted years had to come to an abrupt end and not by choice. There were nights I cried and tried to make understanding of something I had no answers to. But then I quickly realized.

You outgrow people.

I hate it had to come down to what it is, and sometimes I wish I could go back and change it. Because I still miss my friend, very dearly. I still pray for you. I still check up on you when I can. But I asked God for clarity and some of the people who I included in my life's events started disappearing. And the only thing I could do was thank God for favor and guidance.

Do you know that there is someone out there that you don't love yet,
but are supposed to?
You are supposed to cross paths with someone
in a supermarket,
in a drug store,
or in the club,
and love them.
Isn't that a wild thought?
Whether its
romantic
or
platonic.
You are meant to love them.
There are souls that you are meant to touch,
and there are souls that are meant to touch you,
and you have not even crossed paths yet.

Openminded

I made a home out of him.

Did you know that you could make homes
out of people?

You water the flowers.

You clean the dishes.

You mop the floors.

You take care of your home.

Just like you take care of your own.

I created a safe space within him that would be damaging if he
decided to hire a real estate agent.

Move away?

From my home?

After I have spent all of this
time
and money
and energy
and love
and sacrifices

For my home.

I think not.

54

My Love, My Love.

He was soft. Gentle. Kind. He was all of the things I thought described love. He looked at me like he saw me. It was summertime and we were at a friend's pool party. I knew a guy I had past relations with would be there, and I knew how upset he would be if he saw us conversing, so I tried to keep him at an arms length.

It was an awkward scene. Everybody was in bathing suites but no one would get into the pool. People were just standing around talking and it wasn't that many of us so you could hear everyone's conversations pretty well.

I went inside the pool house and he was sitting towards the back with his friends just laughing so I figured he wasn't paying any attention to me. The other guy walks up and began to start a conversation with me and a few of my friends who I was huddled around with.

I tried to look over my shoulder to make sure he wasn't paying attention because I didn't want to get into an argument about why I was speaking to him. A few moments later as the conversation was starting to quiet down I quickly looked over and noticed him noticing me. I knew he was upset so I walked over there to try to ease the tension. We were around people so I know we wouldn't make a scene however I didn't want to make him uncomfortable.

Shortly after that we leave and we're in the car and it's silent. We get home and I say something I knew would trigger a response. "Why were you talking to him anyway?" he says. It hadn't dawned on me that when you're in a relationship with someone you shouldn't dictate who they do and don't talk to so my response really didn't suffice because I was speaking with emotion and not logic. A lot of our problems were unnecessary but necessary to happen. Two people in love at 16 years old with very little guidance on what love really is you don't really have that much to go on. But we did our best.

One thing I loved about him was his ability to always look out for me even when we weren't on good terms. He didn't let our circumstance change his demeanor.

A Note

Now that I'm older I see how silly this was. Of course you're going to feel a type of way if your significant other is conversing with an old fling, but its ok and more mature if you don't. There's nothing wrong with friendly conversation. There's something wrong with it becoming more than that. But as you learn and grow in your individuality, learn and grow in your relationships too. Some things aren't worth the petty arguments and limits you place on each other, for what? Are you with someone you can't trust? I understand you don't trust the other person and thats OK too. But if you trust your partner then trust them not to put your relationship in a position where its hard for you to come back from.

Just remember to think wisely, and be wise in the process.

Choices.

I don't think that in order to love it means to care.
I think of love as an action.
Something that you actively decide to do on a daily basis.
If love was just an emotion,
then I would have to love a lot of people that I have cared about.
But I don't think that's the case.
I have made the decision to love you,
the good
and
the bad.
I have bought a stock in your company.
I have done more than follow you on twitter,
or like a post on your Instagram.
I have made a decision that I actively decide
to act on every single day.
So to love me is to do more than to care.
To love me is to do more than like the way I look
or the way I brush my hair.
I want you to **choose** me.
Every day.
I want you to decide to love me,
no matter how far away we may stray.

*I like to not only be loved,
but I like to be reminded of that as well.*

You calm my storms.
I look over in bed to see you sleep and I see peace.
You calm my storms.
I race home to see you because love is love.
You calm my storms.
On days where I am sad I look to you for comfort.
You calm my storms.
Why does this love that we've created supersede any emotion
that we have ever felt for each other?
Because you calm my storms.

Self-Reflection

You know one thing I've always admired about Frank Ocean was his ability to remain in touch with the worlds current events, but to never be in the mix. You don't ever see him in TMZ scandals, or going on twitter rants, you just see him, or you really hear him for that matter, put out music. He has made his music important and nothing else, and I respect it.

Who is your soulmate? Is it yourself? Someone else? A talent you posses? In Frank Ocean's case it's his music. But how do you latch onto a soul, maybe even a soul you've never even met, and not let it destroy you?

The same thing that can be your strength can also be your weakness.

I've been destroyed a few times. But with each time I am reincarnated into something new, something more sustainable. I noticed that when my boyfriend died a few years ago I was destroyed, and I didn't even realize that until 4 years later. Sometimes, it takes time for you to see the damage that was really caused. I knew I was hurt, heartbroken, all that good jazz. But I didn't know that I was merely destroyed. In my own self-destruction I found love. Love for myself, love for others, and just genuine love for everything I encountered.

Did it have to take him dying for me to come to that conclusion? I'm all for growth but why do you have to go through hell and high water to get there? Are those situations really necessary to cultivate you into the person you were meant to be? Can you grow with heartbreak and pain and not let it consume you to the point that that is where you owe your growth?

I have noticed that that in a lot of my growing pains I grew in literal pain. I don't think it always has to be that way, though.

Take some time to self-reflect

I am this way because:

_____

_____

_____

_____

_____

_____

_____

_____

_____

_____

_____

_____

There was a war,
going on in my mind.
I was a knight,
and I had a shield.
My peace was under attack
from something that was within me.
I was the cause
and the cure
to my pain.
How can that be?

Protect me.

Protection isn't just about physical.
I need more than jealousy
or
defending my honor.
I need to know that you've got my back.
That if something tries to come in between our family,
you will kill.
I want to feel covered,
under your umbrella, just like a cloak of invisibility.

Things I've learned so far:

1. Not always getting what we want sometimes saves our ass.
2. Ask others how you make them feel, then take a look at yourself.
3. Just because you do a good deed, doesn't mean you need to be thanked for it.
4. Sometimes the boy who broke your heart saved you in the long-run.
5. Every disagreement isn't an argument.
6. Friends don't keep tabs.
7. Sleep on your frustration or anger before you confront the person.
8. Sometimes everyone will see your vision except the people you care about most.
9. Sometimes you grow apart from people and that's ok.
10. Sometimes those people were once the closest to you and that's ok too.
11. You can control a lot more than you think, none of which are other people.
12. Self-love is full-time job. Daily affirmations are needed.
13. When you become so uninterested in going backwards you will then know you're on the right track.
14. Karma is very real. Don't sleep.
15. Target is the mecca for all things everything. If you need something, Target has it.
16. If you expect the worse the worse will happen. Whatever you deem to be yours is already written.
17. Pray for everyone, including the Devil, he needs it the most.
18. Learn what destroys you, learn how not to desire it.
19. Reciprocation is not guaranteed just because you feel you are entitled to give what nobody asked for.
20. "Yes, he is very dreamy, but he is not the sun, you are." - Christina Yang
21. There will be mountains you can't move.
22. Know how to belong to oneself.
23. Never let anyone make you feel like you are hard to love.

24. Not everyone you lose is a loss.
25. Never deny yourself the right to your own emotions.
26. You don't stop loving someone just because they don't love you back.
27. Just because something is *their* truth, doesn't make it yours.
28. Just because you can empathize with others, doesn't mean the person you're arguing with can.
29. If he asks you why do Black lives matter, don't fuck him.
30. When you learn someones love language, learning how the language in which they receive apologies, heartbreaks, and handle self-doubt is essential.
31. Don't ease yourself of the pain by saying, "he'll be back", because what do you do when he doesn't? Or what will you do when he does?
32. Just because you love him doesn't mean you are meant to be in a relationship with him.
33. You can love people from a distance and it wont hurt as bad.
34. The moment I realized that I was allowed to be other people including myself, whenever I wanted, was the moment I stopped taking shit from other people.
35. When you figure out how to un-love him you might just learn how to love yourself.
36. Just because they don't love you the way you want them to, doesn't mean they don't love you the way they know how.
37. Never shrink yourself to magnify someone else. There's enough room at the table for everyone.
38. Make yourself aware of how you can be a better friend + act on it, your friends will appreciate it.
39. If you move in with your boyfriend, you'll probably realize if you want to marry him in about 3 months or so. Never underestimate the power of seeing someone in their own element.
40. Always allow yourself to feel the pain + let it go.

(Break)

In order to really lose something I think you have to love it more than yourself.
Yes I love you, and yes I want to be with you,
but if you walk out of my life at this very moment my life will continue.
That doesn't mean I wont miss you.
That doesn't mean that I wasn't *truly* in love with you.
It just means I loved myself more than I loved you.
And don't you want to be with a woman like that?
Don't you want to be with a woman who is able to think for herself?
Or are you one of those men that like control?
You want to be the rise and the fall of my life and I don't necessarily agree with that.
I'm a woman who not only believes in my own rights, but stands up for them as well.
So if you are that man that likes control, then I am not the woman for you.

I am not the woman for you.

There are things that I've been through that I want you to avoid.
It has been a journey to realize that I have been the cause.
The amount of self-realization it took to get here
Didn't occur by happenstance.
But more so circumstance.
I have loved and been damaged.
I have damaged and been loved.
There was a time when I was younger when I hated myself.
I could not comprehend why I was not like who I chose to surround myself with.
I wanted to be accepted.
I wanted to *feel* accepted.
I think back to those times and I cry out of thankfulness.
Thankful that I am not who I used to be.
Thankful that I grew out of that and became more of myself intellectually.
What did they have that I could not give to myself?
What didn't I posses that I wanted more of?
Money?
Friends?
It seemed like that was all you really needed in High School to be accepted.
I struggled with the possibility that I might not ever be.
And I had to come to terms with that.

Acceptance.

Beginning to Cope

(circa March 2013)
Seeing a picture breaks my heart,
not hearing your voice tears me apart.
I try to have faith,
I try to be strong,
but without you, it's so hard to keep pushing on.
Distracting myself is only temporary,
for our love for one another was so contemporary.
You taught me how to live and love in every single way,
but without you, I don't know which road to take.
They say trust in God and have faith,
but what am I supposed to do, when he took you away?
Times will get easier, and the pain will fade someday,
but that day is never gonna come, so i will continue to write and pray.
I'm scared to love, what to gain I will not know.
We had a plan, to grow old together,
but this plan of God's I did not know.
I want to see your face, feel your hug, and hear your laugh.
But I have to wait, until God takes me, so we can finish what we had.
You knew how much I loved you, so that makes it easier,
but what makes it hard, is that the pain keeps sinking deeper.
It's only Day 20, but what about day 200?
How I will feel then? Will my happiness ever be uncovered.
Someday there will be a man, who will try to take your place.
But I will introduce him to your picture, and say 'you can share but
not replace'.
I love you so much, and I always will.
Joshua Christian Level, this feeling is making my heart ill.
I beg God to bring you back, since he is the only one who can
retrieve life.
But he isn't gonna do it, because he meant to take your life.
Why? I do not know. But it isn't my place to ask.
I just wanna be with you, is that so bad?

Dear Diary,

I know that I'm young, but I think I know what love is.
My mom said she gets it too so that makes me feel a little better.
His parents want him to be focused on basketball and I get it,
thats his talent and he wants to focus on it too.
I try to support him in every way I know how but I'm in school too
ya know?
We're supposed to be hanging out this weekend.
We don't think his parents will be ok with us going on a date
so he has to tell them that he's meeting up with his friends at the
movies.
I think I want to marry him.
Actually, I know that for a fact.
When we were younger he actually liked my best friend its actually a
funny story.
It wasn't really funny then, but its funny now so I can laugh about it.
I always knew who he was he went to my church growing up.
When him and his family left the church we kind of lost contact, but
we met back up a few years ago at summer camp and now we're
together. I don't know what I'd do if something were to happen to
him. Sometimes I feel that I care about him more than I care about
myself sometimes. I'm not sure, but I think thats how most people
describe what love is.

Why did you die on me?

In Egypt,
the Pyramids are twice as big as anything you've ever seen.
You start to wonder and ask questions
and you even think you've come up with the answers.
But you haven't.

Life works the same way sometimes.
You come across new people,
new experiences,
new feelings,
and you think you've finally figured it out.
But then life reminds you, that you haven't.

HOMESICK

I had always dreamed of elsewhere.
I travelled the world & went searching for something I couldn't quite
put my finger on.
All I found was myself.
All of the countries I visited & I had always made a home there.
I made myself familiar with things so I could get a grip of what was
my new reality.
In Paris, I made the home out of a hostel for a week that had bed
bugs.
With a switch of a room, I made that too, my home.
In Egypt, I made a home out of a resort for the week
that I couldn't figure out how to turn one specific light off
& slept with the light on the duration of my trip.
In Greece, I made home out of a villa that I had no idea what I was
surrounded by, so I laid hungry for hours until I went walking one
night, and found a corner store and ate after what felt like days.
In London, I made a home out of my best friend's apartment in
Croydon & slept my depression away.
In Germany, I made a home out of an Airbnb and stayed with a man
who's flat was so clean I thought he was a serial killer.
Not very often do you come across a man who owns a clean home
and separates their waste from glass, recyclables, and just trash.
In Barcelona, I made home out of a hostel where I slept in a room
amongst men & women,
and at 4am they would burst in the room with sounds like it was
2pm.
I tried to make a home out of everywhere to avoid the homesickness I
would feel when I ultimately moved away from my family in NC.
D.C. was enticing to me. It has its own culture that I was interested
in experiencing.
I visited once on a family trip and since then had dreams of going
back & also making it my home.
A new city, very little friends, a new him.
It was all so new to me.
I lay here and I miss home.
I can't sleep it away like I did in London,
and I can't starve myself like I did in Greece.

This is my home for now until I seek & make a new home elsewhere.
I've learned that to be at home is subjective.
There is a way to always take home with you wherever you go.
I think knowing yourself has a lot to do with how successful you are
in doing so.
Traveling around Europe helped me know myself.
I got to know how to genuinely be alone & be ok with that.
I can book a flight on my own and actually get on the plane.
I can go to the movies by myself, with a box of sour patch kids,
and an angry orchard and enjoy myself.
I have mastered the art of being alone and not always looking for the
company of other people.
Once you master this, it is easier to make your own home, personal.
Home is subjective, being homesick is a sickness that is curable by
the nature of your own truth.
Don't be afraid to step out of your comfort zone,
you may encounter a new home.

Leave what is yesterday in the past,
and what is tomorrow is yet to come.
May the joys of your life be intertwined
with your passions,
and your sorrows be filled
with later days.

Think about a time you experienced homesickness. How did you heal? How did you cope? Release what you thought you knew and accept what actually is. Write it down:

_____

_____

_____

_____

_____

_____

_____

_____

_____

_____

_____

_____

Sign or Initial here

Prayer

Thank you God for who you were to me
and were for me.
You knew what I needed at the time
and you gave me an abundance of those things through her.
You place people in our lives for a reason,
and although people come and go like the seasons,
my appreciation for their purpose in my life is at an
all-time high.
Most times we don't understand why
until later down the road what that specific purpose is.
But in you I put my trust
to relieve the fear of what I do not know.
Now as I continue to grow, may you continue
to place people in my life that will show me you love me,
through them.
- db & nnk

Today I affirm:
- I am beautiful
- I am worthy to receive love
- I am worthy enough to receive respect and also give it.
- I am blessed beyond measure.
- What I put out into the world is what I will receive.

Write down affirmations that you would like to remind yourself to live by:

1. **I am**

_____

_____

2. **I am**

_____

_____

4. **I am**

_____

_____

5. **I am**

_____

_____

6. **I am**

_____

Daily Reminders:

1. Call your mom back
2. Remember to take the chicken out of the freezer to thaw
3. Go to CVS and buy nail polish remover
4. Also remember to buy white nail polish
5. Remember to show effort and you'll receive interest.
6. Perform the whole routine to the live at Roseland version of Crazy
In Love

It's not entirely true that if you don't love yourself then no-one will be able to properly love you.
I'm not sure who came up with that passive aggressive statement,
but some people genuinely are unsure of how to love themselves.
Maybe it was because the love they once received was unhealthy,
or they confused abuse for love,
it could be a number of things.
But instead of trying to convince people that they aren't worthy of love,
introduce them to themselves and the beauty that they radiate.
Theres no maximum age to learn self-love.
Self-love requires daily affirmations and time spent reminding yourself of how special you are.
Life takes you on a journey of the unknown and its easy to get lost along the way.
Self-love is a journey like life itself.
There is no one direction or right way of doing things,
just learn who you are and expand in that.
Live through you.
Experience you.
Be in an abundance of you.

To the young girl who lost her boyfriend:

I can tell you a lot of things, but a lot of them you are going to have to learn on your own because, well, growth.
Growth sometimes' requires discomfort.
And right now you are in a very uncomfortable situation.

This situation is very new, so give yourself some time to heal.
Don't rush it, don't answer people's questions if you don't want to; you don't owe anybody anything. The next few years are pivotal to your growth because every decision you make from this point on matters.
Learn how to separate emotion from logic, and that will take you a long way.

Accept the fact that it's ok to hurt and feel pain, and it's ok to be angry.
But what's not ok are for those emotions to linger because they can take over you.
Give yourself some time to cry, to lounge around and just do nothing.
Figure out ways to release the negative energy so you can embrace the good that's to come even if you don't see it yet.
Good is coming.
I know you may not see it now, but it is.
Don't try to make sense of what's happening, accept the things you cannot change and come to terms what is & it will help you in the long run, too.

Find ways to cope.
What do you like to do when you're feeling sad?
Do you write?
Do you watch your favorite tv show?
Do you like to be surrounded by friends?
Surround yourself with your girlfriends and have a team of people that have your back because you're going to need it.

I know where your head is right now.
You are me 4 years ago.
And so many people reached out to me and I had no idea what they were talking about. None of it made sense to me until years down the

road after I made so many mistakes and found myself even more heartbroken than I was before.

The best advice I can give you right now is to allow yourself to feel. If you try to suppress these emotions and act like this never happened it will do more damage than good.
Like I said, your world may seem like it's ending right now, but I promise you it's not.
Just keep pushing.
You'll look back on this years later and see how far you've come and be grateful that you didn't let this tragedy consume you.

Miss him. Allow yourself to miss him. And you will always miss him. But there will be a time where you don't miss him as much, and that just means you're healing. I'm here if you need me for any questions or advice, I'm just a phone call away.

Have you ever felt pain in your dreams?
Something happens to you
and yet you physically feel it.
Most times when you wake up from a dream,
the clock begins to countdown to the
absence of remembrance.
You begin a race with your own mind.
Trying to pick out the most important parts
in order to comprehend.
What do you do when you stumble across something that you don't
want to remember?
Where do you tuck away that memory?
Where do you tuck away that dream?

DOING LINES.

What are you addicted to? Love and other drugs?

_____

_____

The spirit I feel when I'm motivated is a high that no drug can reach.
The lowness I feel when my dreams seem so far away is a withdrawal
I try to avoid with each reach for fresh air.
You stay down and work so hard you forget to come up for oxygen.
To breathe and take it all in.
You look up and everything around you has changed while you feel
as if you've stayed the same.
The feeling of love is a drug known by the name of dopamine.
But what is the combination to make motivation.
Do you need hydrogen?
With a mix of oxygen?
A hint of oxy and maybe even some marijuana?
I'm not exactly sure.
But what do you do in the moments where you feel like what you
once felt was easily obtainable is now so far you can't even
comprehend what you once wished for?
How do you keep the momentum going in the midst of your break to
breathe again?
How do you remain motivated while free but focused?
What do you do to remind yourself that you are indeed that bitch?

Prayer

Jesus knew Judas would betray him.
So he invited him and all his other friends to witness the drama of it
all unravel.
Just like love & hip hop.
Lord,
Help me quietly slay my enemies just like you did.
Amen.

HOW TO MASTER THE ART
OF BEING ALONE

I only learned how to be alone when I was forced to. I guess that was my lesson. I'm sure I would have learned the same outcome of the lesson later in life, but differently of course. In the midst of my sadness and vulnerability, I became someone who desired to be anything but alone. There was a time where I couldn't fathom the thought of sleeping by myself. I filled my bed with men who I couldn't fall asleep next to. I quickly realized that the reason I was not able to fall asleep was because they weren't meant to be there. When I was alone I felt restless. Dipping myself in anything to bring chaos to keep me entertained. Sometimes the company I kept wasn't even physical company, I just needed my mind to feel busy. It's one thing to be alone but it's another to feel alone. I had to master that art. To be alone but not feel it.

I started off by figuring out what made me happy, or more so entertained. Netflix series or shows with multiple seasons gave me the opportunity to venture into a different reality. Grey's Anatomy was the start of my lonely journey. The death of George O'Malley tore me apart, but I guess that was necessary, too. I began to enjoy going to the movies by myself, taking long drives, going to the bar by myself. I started to really find myself in the midst of being alone.

I had been in a relationship for the last 4 years and once I had entered college I didn't even fully know what the word 'alone' meant. I entered college full of new people, new boys, and new opportunities it hit me all at once and I was taken aback to say the least. I was angry at him for leaving me by myself. I had no idea what I was doing and even after all of the advice I had received it went in one ear and out the other. I felt no one truly understood what I was going through so I didn't think to really listen and take in account to what they had to say.

I got tired of my bed being full of men I did not want. I began to love myself, more. And in order to love myself I had to know myself. And in order to know myself I had to spend more time alone. All of what I did by myself prepared me to leave the country and take on Europe for 4 months by myself. My first solo trip to Dubai was liberating. I remember I was in the car headed to Abu Dhabi on a trip I booked through Viator, which is a trip on a trip website, and I cried. I cried because I had came so far and my journey was still in process. I cried because here I was in a beautiful country, alone, and it was so hard for me to explain to everyone back home what I had seen.

When I had tried to Greece, I spent a few days in Athens before I flew to Santorini for a few days. Athens was exciting and full of life and history. I had watched Hercules a few times and didn't even realize that Mount Olympus was a real thing. Climbing up the mountain to see some of the most beautiful ancient ruins I had ever seen in my life, looking down on Athens alone, I realized then too that my journey was not yet over, but merely just beginning.

In Santorini I stayed in a villa and I had felt very lonely. Of course I was alone, but at this point I knew I had mastered the art and could take on whatever life threw my way by myself. But in this moment I felt so lonely, even almost sad. I couldn't find anything on TV that was in English, and I was hungry and I couldn't find anything local to eat that I would enjoy. It was late at night and from what I had seen in pictures that Santorini was more enjoyable in the day time. So I laid there, in my villa, lonely. It was in this moment too, I learned another thing about being alone. That when you feel lonely it's easier to sleep away the loneliness, but that doesn't mean it's the right thing to do. Face it. Share your loneliness with yourself and give yourself company. Learn that just because you are alone or even feeling lonely it does not mean you have to feel sad.

Mastering this art has helped me tremendously in any relationship I have built. Platonic or romantic. My boyfriend once told me that he admires the fact that I do not need him. Life is great with him, I would even go as far as to say it's perfect, but he understands that I do not need him. I can do anything I want to do without him he is only an addition to what I've already built. And that spoke to me. I am choosing to be here or anywhere for that matter, and if I need to go elsewhere, alone, I can do that, too.

Prayer

Dear God,
I find it funny how sometimes I catch myself being afraid
to ask you to place or point me in the right direction,
because it may cause me to leave people behind
that I'm not ready to let go of just yet.

A list as to what I have to stop doing…
August 2012

1. stop the twitter shit
2. stop giving a fuck to a certain extent
3. learn how to fully trust
4. stop being impulsive
5. stop making assumptions
6. just shut up and listen
7. be in love. it's not that difficult.

5am thoughts

I first tasted depression while living in Milan.
There was a moment
when I slept for dinner.
I'm not sure if I outcasted myself
or if my surroundings did it for me.

Signs of Depression
- sadness*
- loss of interest in normal activities*
- irritability*
- thoughts of suicide or death*
- Dysphoria*
- disturbance of sleep or appetite*
- weight loss*
- disinterest or conflict*
- self-medications*
- tiredness and fatigue*
- decreased energy and focus*
- isolation*
- difficulty sleeping*
- abandoning hobbies*

*what I experienced

free writing

my fear of failure has taken over my thoughts.
self-discipline is something i know i'm in need of;
yet i'm lacking that same quality.
i'm afraid of all of my ideas going to waste.
i'm afraid of all of my passions going to waste.
i'm afraid that *i* will go to waste.
what will happen if i fail?
after all of this time spent
and money wasted
what do i turn to?
who do i turn to?

lets be proactive

how do you know when you're depressed?

how do you deal/cope with it?

what do you do to pull yourself out of it?

Before I listed the symptoms of depression and the ones in which I identified with. Below is how I pull myself out of it:
- Grey's Anatomy re-runs
- munching on sour patch kids
- watching transformers
- cider
- baking sugar cookies
- writing
- realizing that elsewhere is nowhere at the same time

We all get depressed from time to time. Whats important is that we don't stay in our depression.

I find myself in complicated predicaments 99% of the time.
I know what I'm capable of,
I know what qualities in myself that I posses,
I know that I am meant to be something greater than anything I can
even imagine.
So why do we push the agenda that you have to start from the
bottom in order to get to the top?
I see how it's worked for so many people and now others feel as if it's
the only way.
But my bottom is not your bottom.
My bottom is making my own experience,
paving my own way.
What is the pathway to success for you?
What is the perfect timeline until you stop giving your ideas and
dreams to others for an hourly wage and begin to cultivate them for
yourself?
What is the perfect moment?
Is there a perfect moment?
I understand the ideology that sometimes you may be in a state of
discomfort before you reach what you were really searching for.
But how uncomfortable do I have to get to realize I don't know
myself anymore?
This isn't me.
I'm a creative.
I'm capable.
I have honored myself.
How uncomfortable do I need to be
to just go out
and get shit done.

what do you when you've lost yourself?

I think it's very easy to get lost in yourself. I look around and I become amazed at how far I've come with the realization that life is very hard. As easy as it is to become lost in yourself it's even easier to become just lost. I have gone through so many situations in my life to where I could have just given up and ended it. But as you evolve so do your problems. I look back to when I was in high school and I had a total different set of problems than I do now. What played a factor in those problems? Was it my age? My surroundings? Now I'm 22 and it's like my problems have evolved with my age. Do we solve life's hardships by our mental growth? Is it with each age we are more capable to take on a different set of challenges?

When I was 18 I dealt with a death that almost ruined me. When I was 19 I dealt with a heartbreak that almost ruined me, too. When I was 20 I dealt with the changes of new friends, new scenery, and no idea where I was headed after college. When I was 21 I dealt with the idea that I wanted something more out of what was getting. When I was 22 I dealt with losing two friends who meant the world to me. And yet, here I am, almost 23, battling a new set of problems.

Does it ever end, or do you just get better dealing with it?

As I grow older I realize how easy life can just take you out. If you aren't strong mentally its easy to get caught up in what you can't control and focus on what you can.

Notes:

Dear Them,

I know I can be difficult. I know I can be rude. I know I can be an asshole who makes your life a little more complex than it has to be. But *thank you*. Thank you for accepting me and not trying to change the parts of me you don't like. Thank you for protecting me from outsiders who try to come into my life and turn my world upside down. Thank you for sometimes even protecting me from myself.

Over the years, all of our friendships have grown individually and some collectively. Some of you I have even introduced to each other and you have gone on to foster your own friendships while still being able to maintain and nurture our own, and that not everyone can. But you guys have stuck with me through thick and thin and I've never really noticed how important friendship was until now.

I think back to the time when I was in the 4th grade, crying to my mom asking her why the other kids kept making fun of me. They said I had bad breath and I knew I did, but because of the medicine I was taking I couldn't do much to change it. I had a form of ADHD and was on Adderall for a few years growing up. A few of the side effects were a loss of appetite so I would go all day at school without eating anything and that is what caused my breath to smell. I wanted to tell the other kids that it wasn't my fault, but I didn't want people to notice that I was taking medicine. So I kept it a secret and took the bullying. I would even brush my teeth at school during the day but it didn't make much of a difference. I found myself chewing on cough drops & gum to make my life a little easier and that toned down the name-calling. I was so upset because I knew that not taking my medicine wasn't much of an option. But I wanted to be normal. Like the rest of the kids. I wanted to be able to engage in conversation and laugh and joke. I got on the medicine because I couldn't focus in class and wasn't retaining any material. My parents noticed my behaviors and figured the drug would help me focus in class. But the side effects caused my day-to-day life to be a struggle. While I was at school all I wanted to do was school work and nothing else. My teachers had given me the name "social butterfly" and I couldn't be my true self while I was surrounded by the other kids in school. I wanted the other kids to like me & for them to see my real personality. I couldn't be social so the kids at school would call me weird. My appetite was gone so I was picked on for that as well. But my grades were good so I guess the medicine was working. But every time I took the medicine it wasn't until 6pm when the meds started to ware off that I was my true self. My hunger had returned with a vengeance & so did my personality. I wanted to talk and share the experiences at school and conversations I overheard while I was observing. But I took the medicine every morning at 7:30am for the cycle to continue. Until one day I said no more. I had to learn the basic functions of self-discipline.

In middle school, I had always loved cheerleading and wanted to pursue a slight career as I got older in the competitive world. My mom had cheered in college and I would visit my grandmothers house looking through old picture books of her enjoying the same sport I fell in love with. She was my inspiration. I had the dream to cheer for this elite but very expensive competitive team, but my parents couldn't afford it. I went to school surrounded by a bunch of kids with totally different lifestyles than me so I found myself to be the odd-ball most of the time. A lot of the girls around me were having sex and had boyfriends and I wasn't there yet. I shared my first kiss in the 8th grade with a boy who meant the world to me. A great person all-around and didn't introduce me to heartbreak. I shared with my mom the things I knew and wanted to avoid hoping she could provide me with some type of insight. A friend of mine got pregnant that year and that was my first glimpse into what I could say was adult-hood, lol.

In high school I fell in love. I had a few friends carry over into high school from elementary and middle school and we were still close. They were mostly the friends I had built a relationship with over the years at the church I attended. I made a few friends in high school but in some ways I still felt as if I didn't fit in. The other girls were more pretty and more developed and I wasn't yet.

I was impulsive. Talkative. Very social. I went to church more-so for my parents than my own spiritual belief. I figured praise and worship was more so "grown-folk business"; so me and a few of the other kids made a clique of our own. I was already friends with my god-sister and she had friends of her own, but I didn't always get along with them. I was always very selfish with my friendships and I didn't like sharing my friends with their friends. Mediocre rivalries were formed and so were crushes, so Church became more of a meet-up for our clique than actual church. The boy who I really liked, liked a friend of mine, which because of that we ended up not being friends. When he stopped showing up for church and started going to a new one, we then became friends. We went onto be friends as we both entered college, she's my person.

I entered college with the loss of my very best friend. I fell in love with him when I was kid & I didn't even know what love was. But he made things make sense for me. But he also broke my heart. I spent months angry and blaming him for his life being taken; when if I had of paid more attention in church all those years ago accepting his absence might have been much easier. When he died apart of me died with him. I went into college with a smile that hid the soul of a broken teenager. I tried to search for love in everything else but where it actually was and that did some damage to me, too. But in college I truly found myself. I didn't allow anyone else to break me down I did that all on my own, but I also built myself back up. I learned how to be alone and not feel lonely, I learned what self-love truly was and how to reinvent it when I had to also reinvent myself. I was able to keep myself from drowning and learn how to swim again. In college I became a woman and no one else did that for me.

I think about who I was when I was getting picked on in elementary school, or trying to catch up to my friends in middle school, or falling in love in high school, and I miss myself. I miss my old self sometimes. The me who was gullible and believed there was good in everyone and no one could do any wrong. I still think there's good in everyone but everyone is people too and they fuck up sometimes just like the rest of us. But I miss me. Who I was when he was around. I'm a completely different person and yes I've learned to embrace that, but life has an interesting way in making you cold. It's up to you to remain warm.

I wish I was like my dad sometimes.
He likes the cold.
Most times the cold is where I'm able to really think & process things.
Except I hate the cold.
In times where I'm unsure of what to do,
or where to go,
I think about my dad.
And how strong he is.
And how he protects and defends.
The man that I've always wanted was just like him.
Sometimes I get scared too.
Sometimes I want to be cuddled and be told everything is going to be Ok.
But I always have to be strong for everybody else.
I always have to remind someone else you can make it.
But who's gonna be strong for me?
Who's gonna tell me I can make it?

allow yourself to feel the pain + let it go.

I wonder when this will stop hurting.
I've felt this pain for months now and I thought I came to terms with
what this is.
I've spent nights crying & days remembering I just want to know
when the pain will stop.
You seem to have moved on.
Do you think about me?
Do you still think about the times we had? *drake voice*
Have you forgotten what I once meant to you?
I want to contact you and just see how you're doing.
Let you know that I still think about you everyday.
I want you to know that I miss my friend.
But even if you were to tell me let's start over,
I don't think I could let you in my life
to do it again.

Dear old friend,

I'm happy to see that life is treating you well.
Even in my disappointment and distaste,
I could never wish any bad upon you or your life.
You hurt me in ways that I would not wish on my worst enemy.
I trusted you with my fears,
my goals,
and the things I fell short in.
I trusted that you would see me through.
Through the pain sometimes I caused myself,
and the pain I unintentionally caused others.
You knew me better than anybody ever has or
anybody ever will.
I shared with you my darkest secrets,
and I shared with you my biggest goals and dreams.
I didn't foresee our friendship ending,
because it wasn't an option for me.
I apologize to where I failed as a friend to you.
And I hope that you come across a friend,
who loves you the way I do.
Throughout these years of no communication,
I have learned a lot about myself.
I hope that life continues to bless you with an abundance of
knowledge,
strength, and wisdom,
And I hope that you never have to deal
with what you put me through.

After a brief conversation
it stopped hurting.

Thoughts of an Entrepreneur

I wonder will all of this be worth it.
You don't really know if you're moving in the right direction
so you convince yourself that taking a few steps back is the right
answer.
What is an idea if there's no meaning behind it?
The meaning is like the special sauce.
It's the drive that keeps that idea going.
What if you have more meanings than the actual ideas.
How do you put your entrepreneurship to use?
I don't think of entrepreneurship as a 9-5
I think of it more as a 9-9.
It never stops.
You're involved in every position that you've created but delegated to
someone else.
You're told 'no' more times than you're told 'yes' but that is where
your meaning comes into play.
Your meaning is the actual reason that sets you free.
Your meaning makes it all worth while.
In the times that you face your own ideas and they exhaust you,
Remind yourself of your original meaning,
and you will find home.

A story.

I miss the old me.
And I miss Josh.
I wrote to you, ya know.
Before you died.
I wrote you journals that included my thoughts and feelings.
From feelings of happiness and feelings of disappointment.
I had always had certain expectations of you.
An expectation that you would always maintain your end of the
bargain when you decided to love me.
You always lived up to my expectations,
for the most part.
There were times though, when I felt you didn't.
And just like the times when I wanted you to know how much I
loved you,
I also needed you to know when you made me sad.

I documented everything about us as much as I could.
Every game of yours I visited; I kept those tickets.
Every piece of paper I doodled in class, I kept those as well.
I kept t-shirts, poems, and pictures,
I didn't even know that you would leave me so soon but something in
my head told me to keep everything.

The moment you died I prepared myself for your passing.
Before I received that phone call I was scrolling on twitter.
I was downstairs and I heard my mom answer her phone upstairs in
her room.
The vibe of my timeline on Twitter took a shift, but I was still
unaware of what exactly happened.
In that moment I spoke to God.
God had asked me was I ready for what was about to happen?
I had 10 seconds to prepare myself for the changes that life was about
to make.
And then it happened.
~
I wrote you a journal of my favorite quotes to remind you that I loved
you so much.
My grandma wrote in the first few pages to me long before we even
crossed paths, so I wanted to continue it with all its' glory, for you.

I wanted you to always have something that reminded you of me
even when I was gone.

I wish I was able to gift it to you before you left this Earth,
as I planned the next time I saw you.
Instead, I'll gift it to the people who I know cared as much about you
as much as I did,
and it will still be close to home.
We will continue to love each other,
and love you.

My mom used to read me this book when I was younger about a dog
named Elfie who passed away in her sleep.
Her owner loved her very much and she made sure she told Elfie that
she was always loved every night before she went to sleep.
The book was called, "I'll Always Love You",

I'll Always Love You, Joshua Christian Level.

Journal

Journal Entry
April 27, 1999

Tonight it was my night off. I work 3rd shift. It rain the entire time.

Hey sweetie, thats what I called you sometimes.

Honor your mother and your father and thy days shall be longer.

Love,
Grandma

Journal Entry
May 5, 1999

You didn't go to school today you were sick. We spent half a day watching movies.

Love,
Grandma

Journal Entry
May 5th, 1999

    The things I write are written with the hope that you'll better understand someday about what is important. Your mother and I used to go shopping when she was smaller. We didn't always have money but we went just to spend time together. We wanted to try on clothes and test the different cologne. You are a very smart person. Never let anyone convince you otherwise.

Love,
Grandma

Journal Entry
February 5th, 2013

"Something About Me"

*We just got off the phone by the way and I'm waiting for you to call me back.

p.s. We're having breakfast for dinner tonight and I <u>hate</u> breakfast for dinner.

"I'm quirky, silly, blunt, and broken. My days sometimes are dark and my nights sometimes too long. I often trip over my own insecurities. I require attention, long for passion, and wish to be desired. I use music to speak when words fail me, even though words are important to me as the air I breathe. I love hard and with all that I have, and even with all my faults, I am worth loving."

- Dana Grayson

I'll Always Love You,
Noyah

Quote of the day: "Just keep swimming" - Nemo

Journal Entry
February 5th, 2013
7:37pm

"Support"

Sometimes when you need support, you may feel like I don't know what to do or I'm not here for you. To be honest with you, I don't always have the right words to make you feel better. But I do have the arms to give you a hug, ears to listen, and I have a heart; a heart thats aching to see you smile again. I want you to know that I will always be here for you, no matter what. I love you with everything I've got.

I'll Always Love You,
Noyah

Quote of the day: "Faith is the art of holding on to things in spite of your changing moods and circumstances." - C.S. Lewis

Journal Entry
February 5th, 2013
8:50pm

"Being in love is a good thing, but it's not always the best thing."

There are many things below it, but there are many things above it. You cannot make it the basis of a whole life. It is a noble feeling, but it is still a feeling. Now no feeling can be relied on to the last in its' full intensity, or even to last at all. Knowledge can last, principles can last, habits can last; but feelings come and go. And in fact, whatever people say, the state called "being in love" usually does not last. If the old fairytale ending "they lived happily ever after" is taken to mean "they felt for the next fifty years exactly as they felt the day before they were married", then it says what probably never was nor never could be true, and would be highly undesirable if it were. Who could bare to live in that excitement for even 5 years? What would become of your work, your appetite, your sleep, your friendships?

But of course, ceasing to be "in love" need not mean ceasing to love. Love in the second sense - love as distinct "being in love - is not merely a feeling. It is a deep unity, maintained by the will of God and deliberately strengthened by habit, reinforced by the grace which both partners ask, and receive, from God. They can have this love for each other even at those moments when they do not like each other; as you love yourself even when you do not like yourself. They can retain this love even when each would easily, if they allowed themselves, to "be in love" with someone else.

-C.S. Lewis

Quote of the day: "I fell in love with his courage, his sincerity, and his flaming self-respect. And it's these things I'd believe in even if the whole world indulged in wild suspicions that he wasn't all he should be.

I love him and that is the beginning of everything."
-unknown

113

Journal Entry
February 7th, 2013

I have been struggling for the last couple of days about goals, college, graduating high school, and mainly being broke while doing so. My plans of going to some branch of the military are still in effect, but not until after college. I want to cheer, join a sorority, and join ROTC. But am I doing too much? I wish someone would point me in the right direction. I'm scared of life.

Quote of the day: "It is a risk to love. What if it doesn't work out? Ah, but what if it does?" -Peter McWilliams

Poem:

It was casual at first
between you and me.
Introduced at a time
when life was carefree.
You brought me comfort
and put me at ease.
A sensation that felt
like a warm summer breeze.
Whether up or down,
it seemed that you only cared.
But some disapproved
of the bond that we shared.
You laughed at my jokes,
and I laughed at yours,
Our laughter was the key,
that would open up doors,
The time we shared was a delight,
our future was bright.

-Dulcie Ann

Journal Entry
February 7th, 2013

"Glass"

Ya know,
I really feel for like,
girls who get their heart broken.
And I'm not talking about us right now.
This is deeper than us.
This is apart of life.
Boys and girls; it happens to the both of us.
You open your heart to someone and they take you for granted.
Like you were nothing,
like you were just there to pass by time.
That sucks.

Quote of the day: "Fool you made the girl fall in love, you said those beautiful things, she thought you spoke things you mean." - Gavin DeGraw

Journal Entry
February 7th, 2013

Quote of the day:

"I am a day of the week,
maybe a Tuesday
        fresh and forgettable.
But if I am a Tuesday,
then you are a Friday.
        yearning and slow,
And while people live through me,
they anticipate you.
And we could never be together,
because brash doesn't belong with bashful,
and Friday never held Tuesday's hand."

- Anonymous

Journal Entry
February 7th, 2013

If you noticed, I've taped down some of my old thoughts in this journal for you to read. Some from '09, '10, '11, but they are old. Things have changed. It's just to give you some sort of idea of who I am, or well, who I was.

I don't want you to be scared, or leave me. I just want to open myself up to you in a way that you may have not seen before.

And if you already knew, thats good too.

I'll Always Love You,
Noyah

Quote of the day: "You are not a bad person, you are a very good person who bad things have happened to." - Sirius Black

Journal Entry
February 9th, 2013

Well, we just left cotillion practice and now we're at your grandma's and you're taking a nap. I really want to take a nap but I can't because I have to study so no nap for me.

I'll Always Love You,
Noyah

Quote of the day:
"The saddest kind of sad is the sad that tries not to be sad. You know, when sad tries to bite its lip and not cry and smile and go, 'No, I'm happy for you.' Thats when it's really sad." - John Mayer

Journal Entry
February 9th, 2013

"After A While"

After a while you learn
the subtle difference between
holding a hand and chaining a soul.
And you learn that love doesn't mean leaning,
and company doesn't always mean security.
And you begin to learn that kisses aren't contracts,
and presents aren't promises.
And you begin to accept your defeats,
with your head held high up,
and your eyes ahead,
with the grace of a woman,
not the grief of a child.
And you learn to build all your roads on today,
because tomorrow's ground is too uncertain for plans,
and futures have a way of falling down mid-flight.
After a while you learn all that you can really endure;
that you are really strong and you really do have worth.
And you learn and you learn,
with every good-bye you learn.

-   Veronica A. Shoffstall

Quote of the day: "If you don't feel it, flee from it. Go where you are celebrated, not merely tolerated." -Paul F. Davis

Journal Entry
February 19th, 2013

I haven't wrote in a long time because I haven't been really happy with the way our relationship was going. I didn't know what to say if I wrote. Now that I've had time to clear my head, I think I have the words, well the right words, to say.

You know I love you, the world knows that. And if somebody were to say I was lying they are sadly mistaken. Throughout these last few years I have gotten to know you inside and out. Up and down. Vertically and horizontally. I can honestly say I know you. I get so nervous sometimes thinking to myself what girl could possibly fill my shoes? What girl can love you like I do and 100 times more and better? And I can honestly say, nobody.

Even though you may find a girl that you think loves you even remotely close to me you are very wrong. I would go to the moon and back for you. I would do anything you ever asked. You needed me at a game I'd find a way to get there. I wanted to make you feel loved. I wanted you to know that you were loved. I wanted you to know that I wasn't going anywhere. And no matter what I would always be there for you. But I can't do that anymore. I can't give you all of me if I'm not even receiving part of you. You may say you're doing the best you can well are you really? I'm not one to say that someone isn't good enough, but damn. Material things are not my forte. I've never asked, never even thought about it. It wasn't because I didn't think you could provide that it was because because I simply didn't want or need it. All I wanted from you was consistency. One day you would treat me like I was the luckiest girl on the planet and the next day I second guessed everything you ever told me based off of how you made me feel. I wasn't able to see you on Valentines day and that was really hard for me. Mainly because I had this image of what I wanted and I got nowhere close to that. When you told me that you and Kanayo went to the Apple store for the longest time it just made me think. And that day I had so many emotions going through my head...

Journal Entry
February 20th, 2013

You died today.
Well, yesterday.

R.I.P Josh Level
May 22nd, 1995 - February 19th, 2013

Rubber Ducky Dracula
I am still at a loss for words.
A part of me is angry,
and a part of me is so very sad.
You were my everything,
& you meant the world to me
You loved me no matter what,
flaws and all.
And for that I am grateful.
I will continue to write to you,
I will never stop,
I hope you will look after me in heaven.
say hi to my dad for me.
I am so glad you finally have the opportunity to meet him.
I bet he loves you.

I'll Always Love You,
Noyah

Quote of the day: "I've found a love greater than life itself." -Joshua
1:8

Journal Entry
March 17, 2013

"I think I'm ready now"

It's almost been a month.
I'm trying to write this without crying,
but it's difficult.

"Young love is innocent, young love is us." - Gavin DeGraw

I miss you so much, words cannot explain.
Once minute I'm happy,
and the next I'm super sad.

I wish I could hear your voice, hear you laugh.
I need you, I miss you, I love you.

Come back.

Journal Entry
June 4th, 2013

"I'm not afraid of dying, I'm afraid of old age"
-unknown

"12am her mind wanders,
she tends to think about something that happened
5 years ago, or something that happened 2 hours ago,
or something that could happen 10 years from now.
Her mind is like a hurricane,
its a wreck.
It's full of beautiful yet awful thoughts.
It's 1am and her mind continues to wander."

-A.E.

I had sex with someone else today.
I'm looking for you in other guys.
That's not ok.

I'm sorry.

Journal Entry
June 8th, 2013

I graduate high school today. It's been a long four years and 95% of that time was spent with you. I walked around your house in your jersey that you gave me today the "team loaded" one and it smelt just like you. I smelled it over and over again because who knew that one simple smell could bring back so many memories. I miss you dearly and I can feel you watching me all the time. I wish I could see you, hug you, kiss you, and best of all smell you. My life is about to change dramatically. I'm about to go to college. Unfortunately without you which isn't what we all planned to do so that is a major setback. I know you're proud of me and I find comfort and joy in that. I cannot wait to start this 4-year journey with you again.

Rubber Ducky Dracula. I'll be home soon.

I'll Always Love You,
Noyah

Journal Entry
November 9th, 2013

This has been by far one of the longest few months in my life. I went through a terrible heartbreak. I thought this guy cared about me when I was really just a game. No literally, he told me that to my face that he enjoyed hurting me and that he never cared about me in the first place. I have never went through so much pain. I've lost friends and I've made some, but most importantly I began to find myself and I'm still not done. I have felt so alone lately and all I do is pray for better days. I miss you deeply. I saw a video that someone posted of you yesterday and I heard your laugh for the first time in almost 9 months. It's contagious. I need healing, and strength, and courage. In order to survive I need those things and more. I feel like I'm losing here.

I'll Always Love You

Quote of the day: "I learned a lot about falling in love when I fell out of love and I learned a lot about being a friend when I was alone." - unknown

Journal Entry
January 4th, 2014

I'm sorry I've been so distant. I honestly don't know what to say. I've gotten my heart broken for the 2nd time in 6 months. I get so angry with you sometimes because you left me. If you were here none of this would be happening to me. You left me. I needed you. I still need you. I'll always need you. I wish I knew what you were thinking, how you're doing, what you're feeling.

I'm still in love with you. But I don't want to be. The pain of missing you is so unbearable. I can't allow myself to feel it. I have a fear of being alone. I've been with you for so long, I don't know how to do it. Can you please come back?

I'll Always Love You

Quote of the day: "I am trying to remember you and forget you at the same time." -unknown

Journal Entry
February 14th, 2014

In 5 days it will be a year since we last spoke. Time has flown by so fast and I miss you more than ever. As I sit here and write to you, I am waiting to be somewhat "surprised" by my supposed "Valentine". Even though I don't really like him anymore. In my relationship with him I have somewhat, well no, I have settled. I have received less than what I deserve, and less than what you've given me when you were here, and I have just recently figured out that I was so sick of it. So that is really my Valentines gift: realization.

I have started to fall out of love with you. Even though I will always love you I'm not sure if I can be "in love" with you. Mainly because I shouldn't be in pain when I am in love with someone. I still have the rose you gave me and the gift you made me for last Valentines day. I read it all the time. I miss you with all my heart. And I can't wait until the day we meet again.

I'll Always Love You

Quote of the day: "Only for you, theres no one else I'll give my heart and my time to. I believe in us and I know you do too, and if you're down for me I'. down for you. Always I love you." -Josh Level

Journal Entry
September 12th, 2015

I'm frustrated with myself.
I may need a therapist.
I always run people away and I don't know whats wrong with me.
It hurts me and makes me extremely sad.
I don't want to keep doing this.
I'm fed up.
Every time something almost good happens to me I ruin it.
Between my overthinking and dramatic ways,
I'm not sure whats the issue.
I want to have a real relationship with someone one day.
But I'm never gonna let that happen.
How are you not here but you effect my everyday life.
My habits, my insecurities, my emotions are still haunted.
I just wanna be normal.

I'll Always Love You

Journal Entry
October 18th, 2015

I'm not sure how to explain this situation but I'm going to try my best.
I met a guy, and he was great.
But it was forced.
And its hard for me to admit that because I really wanted it to work.
But I'm not sure if I wanted him to work as much as the idea of us together.
I do not understand why I'm so upset because I wasn't happy.
I wanted more.
I wanted better,
and he couldn't give it to me.
I don't want to accept the type of "love" he was giving me because I know I didn't deserve it.
I just don't know what that was.
I don't want to think about him anymore.
I don't want this anymore.
I want to be happy.
But I need patience for what I truly want.
Patience….

I'll Always Love You

Quote of the day: "We accept the love we think we deserve." -Perks of Being a Wallflower

~

After Josh died I really struggled to find my identity.
I gave my heart and body to boys who only wanted me until the morning.
After that, my well-being wasn't their responsibility.
I entered college with expectations
and it seemed as though I kept rooting against myself judging by all the crappy situations
I found myself in.
I loved and I lost but that's apart of life right?

I had dreams about him ever so often.
Maybe once in every 6 months.
I had a specific dream about him a few years ago.
I was in the process of really moving on and one of my biggest fears was knowing if he would have moved on too.
In my dream he a had a completely new set of friends.
They would play basketball together, hang out and I was happy for him.
I was passing by him at the movies and in that moment I wanted to be happy for him
but I was still so very sad.
He came up to me and he said,
"I'm ok Noyah. It's ok if you move on. I have new friends now, and they're good for me. I still love you, I will always love you, and that's ok."
I haven't had a dream about him since.

A short story
(circa 2010)

You start off as a kid, then you go to a big-kid, then you go to a preteen, then a teenager, an adult and so forth. The cycle of life is one of the most amazing wonders of the world. We haven't quite worked out the kinks of it, but humanity is slowly working its way up there. Your teenage years are one of the most memorable, most extreme and exotic years of your whole life! But it can also be one of the most life altering.

When I was twelve, my best friend and I considered that twelve to be a "pre-teen" age. We felt that we were one step closer to being a teenager, we practically felt like we were twenty going on twenty-one, and we were about to reach the legal drinking age. But not quite. We both had no idea that the responsibilities as a teenager were so demanding, we thought we were about to run wild and naked through the streets. we had no idea about sex, boys, and backstabbing friends. But we quickly found out that it was us against the world.

I was twelve, in the sixth grade, and my name is Rebecca, Becca for short. I attended a prep school, which is for gifted kids, and of course I was on the honor roll. I had buck teeth, a huge overbite, and short hair. I was liked by many, hated by a few. But the few that hated me didn't phase me. My mom's name was Jackie, and my step-dads name was Oliver. I had little sister, Karen, and an older brother, Max. I never really talked to my real dad, Jeff, very much. But when I did, I enjoyed it a lot. My dad didn't live in the same state my family lived in because he moved away for his job a couple of years ago. My dad and I always had plans of one day him taking me to Paris, and we would just spend lots of time together. I was always used to him making promises and breaking them, but this one promise, something was just telling me to believe him.

I wouldn't understand why my dad did the stuff that he did. I always felt confused when she talked about him. But one thing I knew I would never be confused about is that I loved him. My dad and I never had a strong relationship. We just kind of went with the flow. We fussed, fought, argued, and disagreed. But I never understood why he never came to see me. I remember when it was my mom, my step dad and I. And we used to live in the old house before we moved into the new one. My mom would tell me a couple days before that my dad was coming to see me. I would get so excited that I would anticipate seeing him. One day he was supposed to arrive at my front door and he didn't show up. Again, I could hear my mom on the phone arguing with him in the other room about why he cant come. It was always some lame excuse. Something I've of course, heard before. "I got called in by my job", or, "I couldn't drive all the way there this time". I, being twelve, know the difference between an excuse and a lie.

Heartbroken, sad, and confused, I knew he wasn't coming. The look on my moms face, I could read it all. She said "I'm sorry, but your dad couldn't make it this time." I wanted to cry, but I was too angry to cry. I was angry at him for not trying hard enough to come and see me. I was angry at my mom because she should have made him come. And I was angry at my step dad, because he was here and not Jeff.

— —

Its report card day and it's the last semester of sixth grade. I was officially tired of being picked on by the eighth graders and I couldn't wait to pick on some sixth graders when I was in the 7th grade. And I would do the same thing to the 7th graders when I was in the eighth grade. Waving my report card around in the air as I rushed to the bus, it was about to slip out of my hand, and the wind would carry this honor roll away out of my reach. All A's and B's on my report card and I had no problem flaunting it in the other kids faces. As I approached the bus to climb up the accumulating steps I skipped to my seat with joy and gladness anticipating my parents faces when I show them this awesome report card. I was so ready to go home and call Jeff, my dad, and tell him about the victory. Whenever I got good grades he would send me something in a package from where he lives filled with lots of goodies and treats. He even told me that I would get money depending on how many A's I got, and since my report was filled with most of them, I just had to get home and call him. We moved into a new house now, so I'm still learning my address so I can tell him where to send the goody package.

The bus approached my home with a loud screech of the tires and I rushed off to run to the new house. I came inside, only to find my little sister watching SpongeBob on the couch, and my parents talking outside on the back porch. My step-brother didn't live with us. He was Oliver's son, so he also had his own mommy. Just like Karen and I have Jackie our mom. Max comes to visit every once in a while. Like for Christmas or Thanksgiving. But he doesn't actually own a room in our new house because he isn't here everyday. I peaked outside the window and it looked like my parents were having a pretty serious conversation. A tear rolled down my moms face and anguish took over my dads emotions. It was written all over his face. As they walked inside, I knew something very bad was about to happen.

"Come up stairs, Becca. We have something very important to talk about with you."
"Can I come too mommy?", Karen shouted.
"No, not this time sweetie," said my mom with this blank expression on her face.
She looked like she was holding back millions of tears that were about to burst from her eyes. As we entered my parents room Oliver shut the door and my mom told me to come cuddle on the bed with her. My heart dropped as coldness filled the air. I had absolutely no idea what was going on. But I guess I was about to find out.
"Rebecca, today we spoke to your aunt, and today she informed us that your dad, Jeff, was in a motorcycle accident."
I thought to myself, 'oh just a car accident. He's gotten into of those before and was just fine'. But the look on my mothers face didn't read that this time.
"Jeff was in the hospital, and he was in serious condition. He didn't make it." He finished. That was it. He didn't make it. I didn't understand what those words meant.
I was quiet, but because I had nothing to say. I couldn't cry. I didn't feel like crying. I couldn't make any emotion. Any sound. I was blank. My mom told me to "say something", but nothing could come out. They asked me if I was ok. I said yes, and I walked out of their room, went into mine, and I went to sleep.

Next thing I knew, I was in the car with my mom and her friend on the way to the mall to pick out a "funeral" outfit. It still hadn't occurred to me that my dad had died. It hadn't fully registered into my brain. My mom was pulling out dresses left and right asking if this was ok, and did I think it was pretty? I went up to her with this really skimpy dress and said, "Is this ok?" She said, "No honey, that is not okay to wear to your father's funeral," I thought to myself, "funeral?". And then it hit me. On the ride back, I took a look outside of my window up at the stars and I said, "oh my gosh, he's really gone." It finally hit me that I can never see him again.

My dad told me that one day he'd take me to Paris, so we could spend lots of time together. He promised me a lot of things. He promised that he would come and see me, but I was stuck waiting for a man that would never show up. But my dad me the biggest promise of them all, that he would be there for me, but he lied again. He's gone, and my life is about to change forever.

Thinking back to what I went through in the past years I might say I've become a better person. You could say I've matured a little bit, and just like every other teenage girl my body has changed a lot. Oh what a joy that has been. I was thirteen about to be fourteen in the 8th grade. Still a kid, others in my grade were called "grown", I was the exact opposite. I have friends who are engaging in sex, but I was in the 8th grade and didn't really care what sex was.

The hallway was very hectic, loud, and so many people. Black. white, hispanic, and asian. All different races surrounded me. It didn't really bother me. Was it supposed to?

"Excuse me", some random girl asked, "What page did Mr. Barkley say to turn to?"

I'm thinking in my head, "How should I know? I wasn't paying any more attention to that teacher than you were.

"I don't know", I answered.

As I was listening to the conversations that surrounded me, people were talking about things that I didn't even know existed. One time, I was overhearing my two friends having a conversation about the number 69. I asked what that number was just curious as to why it was so significant. And she told me it was a sex position. I didn't even want to know anymore about it then they had already told me.

When I got home from school, I came home early to a dirty house which I was expected to clean. Unfortunately, my mom expected me to come home everyday and do ALL of my chores. This includes: vacuuming, cleaning the kitchen, using tiles on the bathrooms, clean my room, and do it all before both of my parents come home, I can't just come home everyday from a long 8 hours of school and she just expects me clean. When I heard of this rule, I was livid. i sometimes kept my room clean and my mom always had to come back behind me and tell me what I did wrong or how I didn't do it the way she liked it. Me, being thirteen, all of what she was saying, was kind of irrelevant to me. I loved my mom, I really did. The truth was, she was a mom, and that was it.

—

My step-dad Oliver and I always had a special relationship. He was basically there for me when Jeff was not. He, also from the help of my mom, taught me right from wrong. He taught me how a guy should treat a lady, and what not to eat on your first date. Oliver and I had our own special bond. He would literally take me on a father-daughter dates, and he would show me exactly how my official first day, with a real boy, was supposed to be like. Oliver was the type of guy that was very down to earth. I would never actually call him Oliver though, I would simply call him "dad". I called my real dad, Jeff. I did this because, the definition of a dad was very special to me. A dad is someone who is there for you no matter what. Who comes to all of your basketball games and just supports you in every way that he can. Well since I am a daughter and not a son, a dad shows me what a man should do to women, and be a man also. But Oliver fit that definition almost perfectly, and that is why I called him, "dad".

There was a time when I was supposed to be having the best time of
my life.
I was traveling from country to country,
one week I was in Paris,
the next I was in Egypt.
But what a lot of others don't know, is that I dealt
with a very serious case of depression during that time.
After all of the heartbreaks and losses I had experienced up until this
point,
you would think that it would be a walk in the park for me to be a
lone.
But I struggled with it daily while I was studying abroad.
Now I realized that a lot of my depression has more so to do with
not partaking in activities that I would usually immerse myself in
while I was home.
I mean,
while I was living in Italy I had a total different life.
New friends. New food. New daily routine.
To some that sounds exciting, as it should.
Because who wouldn't want to pack up and move to a new country to
start over?
I did, and I wanted to enjoy it, but I couldn't.
I found it very difficult for me to connect with other people.
There wasn't many others that looked like me so I struggled with
making and maintaining friends.
So that took a toll.
Before I left for Italy, I had this pre-conditioned idea that Italy was
mostly fettuccini Alfredo.
I was wrong.
So that took a toll as well.
Simple, I know, but I'm a picky eater and 95% of the menus were in
Italian,
and because I spoke no Italian and I wasn't taking an Italian
language class, I was kinda stuck.
I was always eating four cheese pasta, which got really old, very
quickly.
I struggled with some money problems as well so even though I tried
to make the best out of my experiences and finessing, that took a toll,
too.
There was 10 days I didn't leave my apartment.
I didn't go to class, I stayed in the bed all day with the blinds closed,
and barely ate.

I couldn't put into words what was wrong with me.
Here I was, in one of the most amazing countries, and I'm wasting it away in the bed.
The locals looked at me weird because I didn't look like them, and the students in my program were difficult to connect to because we didn't have a lot in common.
I missed my friends and family back home,
and I spent most of my days applying for jobs. I was about to graduate and I had no idea
what in the hell I was about to do, so that took another toll. I just knew I wanted to move out of North Carolina, I wanted to move away from home when home is what I'm currently longing for.
So I was sad.
Usually when I'm feeling sad I familiarize myself with things I know that make me happy,
and since I couldn't walk to the local corner store and buy some sour patch kids,
or bake some sugar cookies, or just go home and hug my mom,
I had to really learn how to pull myself out of my own sadness.
I became close with one of my classmates and we had a lot in common.
We ended up traveling to Barcelona, Egypt, and and Germany together.
The times that I was with her I would actually put on some make up and do my hair.
Before, when I was feeling sad, I had a hard time looking in the mirror because I knew I wasn't living up to the physical expectations that I had set for myself.
But she helped pull me out of my sadness, too.
Thank you, Sharoyal.

A Better Understanding

to deal with your own depression already is struggle,
but to recognize, deal, and protect someone you care about from their
own
is a total different story.

depression may not even be the exact word.
its not diagnosed, it was more so a feeling of overbearing sadness
when you are unaware of how to deal with your own emotions.

i didn't know what was going on.
we weren't really seeing eye to eye so I thought I had personally
caused you
to distance yourself from me.

typical conversations became arguments,
and that got old, very quickly.
i swiftly noticed that you were dealing with something more
then I could take accountability for.

your tone was different, and so were your daily moods.
one minute you were all laughs and smiles,
and the next you completely shut down.

i suggested that we bake cookies,
because i knew that made you feel better.
i also suggested that you talk to me,
because i was going crazy.

my mistake was that i made your depression about me
more than it was about you.
and i'm sorry for that.

i wanted you to feel better for me.
i couldn't sleep knowing you were hurting,
so i wanted you to *be* better for me.

i argued with you completely disregarding
any of the signs you showed me that
you were sad.

and instead of trying to figure out why you were sad and how to fix
it,
i spent more time trying to figure out how i made you feel sad,
and convincing you to leave until you weren't sad anymore.

i had to check myself.

—

the truth is,
when you're effected by something, so am i.
i can act like it doesn't, but thats not the truth.
i had to learn how to not take it personally.

i would be lying to myself by saying that your depression doesn't
effect our relationship.
because it does.
but that doesn't mean that I'm not there for you
even until you're ready to talk about it.

you spoke to me with the intent to share.
you poured out your fears and your wishes
and i listened with an open-mind.

i wanted to remind you how special you were,
that this too shall pass.
that we have all gone through and experienced
what you're allowing to take over your thoughts and feelings.

i had to learn how to be patient.
that understanding the causes and effects of what was affecting you
doesn't make me selfish,
it just makes me aware.

i told your friends who knew you best to reach out to you,
i didn't know what else to do.
i just wanted you to know that you had people who cared about you.
i wanted you to be reminded that you were not in any of this alone.

i believe that when you love someone, you love them even when they
are not the easiest to love.

you protect them as much as you can even if that means protecting
them from themselves.
if i could take away all of your pain and troubles i would.
but i couldn't do it.

you wouldn't be the man you wanted to be if i stood in the way of
the life lessons meant for God to teach you.
so i let you deal with it and i protected you from what i felt was
detrimental.
even if that means it was me not being as understanding as i could,
so i changed my outlook.

now, you speak more.

a memory of anger

I wanted to make him hurt like he made me hurt.
I wanted him to feel the pain that I felt.
My body had never been touched before because I was saving it for you.
You were supposed to protect me from harm when it turns out that that harm *was* you.

—

I look back and think about the boy I gave my virginity to.
It was supposed to be you, y'know?
Luckily, I had enough courage to tell you the mistake I had made,
and you forgave me,
how were you so brave?

—

I look up to the heavens and I thank God because he graced you with forgiveness.
If the roles were reversed I don't think I would have had the strength to do it.
I lost my virginity not because I loved him.
I lost my virginity because I knew losing it to anyone but you, would hurt you,
and that was so selfish of me.

—

In my head,
I figured it would make up for the hurt you caused me with that girl.
You didn't even have sex with her,
but you made her think that you loved her,
and that broke me to pieces.

—

He was there and you weren't.
Some would say he used me but I technically used him.
I'm still sorry about that.
I was wrong to lay down with him.
I was wrong to intentionally want to hurt you.
I was just wrong.

—

But still,
you forgave me.
You loved me and accepted my wrong-doing.
You welcomed me with open arms and overlooked my mistake.

In that moment I realized I didn't deserve you.
But you gave me your heart anyway.
I never dropped it since then.
Thank you for loving me regardless of the mistakes I made.
You represented God's ability to forgive.
Through you, I learned the true definition of Grace.

Pieces of me,
Given to,
Pieces of you,
Never made any of us,
Whole.

Closing

Now Playing: "Oh How It Hurts" - Barbara Mason

I guess I say all of this to say,
life is hard as fuck.

I thought after Josh died I would never love the same again, and part of me was right. The next time I fell in love it was totally different than anything I had ever felt before. This time, I fell in love with his ability to love me regardless of what I have been through. I tried not to make that love too important at first, but I couldn't help it. I had never dated a man with a different religion than me, and I think of my relationship with God being more spiritual, because to me, religion is man-made. But our difference in belief systems never really played a factor in the relationship that we built, I don't have any advice for you on that just yet, though, just that it's possible.

Throughout my relationship, I started to do a play-by-play of my past relationship and college situationships in my head to see where exactly I went wrong. My freshman year I met a boy who showed me that just because you are able to empathize, everyone did not possess that ability. I also met a boy who throughout his inability to see my worth, I learned what it actually was and what I didn't want it to be. Towards the end of that year year I met a boy who taught me things about sex that I had never heard of, things that I quite enjoyed.

My sophomore years' love interest was someone who I had known all of my life. I found myself to always have been in love with him. Ya know the love where your parents are really close with his parents and you guys are sorta cousins but not really? Yea, I was on that type of shit. But by the end of that year I quickly realized that just because you are familiar with someone doesn't mean that you have to be involved with them & their familiarity.

Junior year I thought I was ready to date again but I lied. I wasn't. I enjoyed being single and keeping my options open. I really really cared about this guy though, and I knew that with time spent and dedication we could actually be something. With this guy I learned that not everybody wants to learn about you, so stop explaining yourself and convincing them to. The right guy who is meant to love you will want to learn your every detail, and it stressed me the fuck out why he didn't take the time to really *know* me.

By senior year I was full-blown doing my entrepreneur shit so I didn't even entertain any guys. I went and lived in Italy for a few months and forgot what sex felt like while I was gone. I was so busy sightseeing and fighting depression I forgot for a second what it felt like to be touched, and loved. Everyone that I had loved dearly was thousands of miles away from me and it was like I was learning to love myself from scratch, except in complete silence and solitude. When I got back to the States, I was focused on graduating but I had met someone on the internet the day before I came back home. Who knew that I would also make a home out of him.

Those 4 years in college flew by so quickly. I just remember my freshman year before I even moved into my dorm, met and lost my person, and experienced more heartbreak than I think the average 20-something has ever dealt with. But someone told me that it would happen like this. Not exactly like this, but they expressed to me to take my time and to not rush things. I think I did a pretty good job of taking my time in college, but I happened to rush almost every relationship that I started to form. Truth is, I wasn't ready yet. It took me almost 3 years to fall out of love with my dead boyfriend and when I finally did I met someone who turned my world upside down. I met someone who allowed me to really know myself while trying to get to know him. I met someone who when I think of the future they're not too far behind me. I met a man who I see myself in. Who just wants to change the world and inspire everyone he comes across. But the fact is, he inspires me.

I've always made it a point to tell anyone who asks me for advice that growth is uncomfortable, and growing with someone is even more uncomfortable. A lot of us want love but have no idea what it actually takes to sustain that love you want so bad, and I've only reached the surface of it. I think to be in love with someone and to be in a relationship with them are two different things, just like I think unconditional love and unconditional relationships are two different things. I can choose to love you even when I do not like you. But I cannot choose to be in a relationship with you if you do not meet the requirements and expectations that I have set forth as a romantic or platonic partner. Feelings change, just like C.S. Lewis said, your feelings will change, they always will. Just as you can choose to be in love with him you can choose to be in love with somebody else, and the quicker you accept that the easier it will be for you to continue to make that choice.

My 5am thoughts are what drive my spirit throughout the day. I am able to clearly think and reinvent myself as I process my experiences or the experiences made up in my head. What is 5am meant for? You spend 7-9pm the night before preparing for the next day, and you spend 7-8am that morning getting dressed ready to take it on. But what about 5am? Everyone seems to forget about it. I am truly thankful for 5am because the voices in my head are completely different at 2pm. It is ok to reinvent yourself. It is ok to take care of yourself. But most importantly, it is ok to not only love yourself, but like yourself.

Ending - A Note

I thought the book was over, but over these past two weeks I have
learned something about myself that this book wouldn't be complete
if I didn't tell you. When I started writing this book 2 years ago, and
this specific copy, (because I've started this piece of work multiple
times over the last few years), I realized that I was not a storyteller. I
cannot make up a plot with a climax, a downfall, create characters,
kill them off, and create new ones like Shonda Rhimes. That is not
my writing style. The only way I can write and write effectively is in
stanzas, poetries, and short stories where I do not have to hide
behind a character to share my truth. But with this, I am able to
share short stories and poems about what has ever happened to me,
because it *has* happened to me. I wanted this book to be for women
and for women only. Empowering them through the trials and
tribulations that I have been through and understanding that this was
my coping mechanism while encouraging them to find their own. The
journal exercises are ways for you to contribute your thoughts in a
book of thoughts, and to visually understand and grasp what you are
reading and going though to figure how to write it all down. This
book lacks complete organization but so are my thoughts at 5am.

Over the last few weeks I have been feeling uninspired and overall
just tired. I'm not necessarily sleepy because for the past few months
I have been sleeping away my disappointment. The disappointment
that I feel is disappointment in myself. My inability to maintain some
type of stability in my job life sends me into a depressive state that
causes me to lack inspiration in all of my entrepreneurial efforts. The
idea of working a job to pay a bill doesn't make a lot of sense to me.
Some, like my parents, may argue that I am immature and always
preparing myself for instant gratification. But I look at the decisions
that I've made in terms of setting myself up in the future for
something greater than myself, and that is the exact opposite of
instant gratification. My 5am thoughts are more emotional based, but
what are my midday thoughts? When I wake up in the morning and I
take on yet another day, it's like my thoughts at 5am disappear.

What do I think about in the middle of the day, on my second and
final 15 minute break, from an 8 hour shift?

What do I think about then?

Notes:

_____
_____
_____
_____
_____
_____
_____
_____
_____
_____
_____
_____
_____
_____
_____
_____
_____
_____
_____
_____
_____
_____
_____
_____
_____

Notes:

_____
_____
_____
_____
_____
_____
_____
_____
_____
_____
_____
_____
_____
_____
_____
_____
_____
_____
_____
_____
_____
_____
_____
_____
_____
_____
_____
_____

Anxiety: A short film

I've been in my head for the longest; overthinking things so much that it got me to the point where it feels like my world is falling apart.

The constant manipulation that I fight with everyday in my head, it's starting to feel like my thoughts have won the battle.

I feel like the weakest soldier on the battlefield; I keep fiddling and losing focus on destroying because I'm so distracted. I get up everyday out of bed, I doll my face up, and I go into a new day where I have to pretend that everything is ok when I know it's not.

I've been challenging my own mind and getting angry with myself because I'm not where I want to be, and who I want to be.

~

There's a lot of demons that I fight with everyday, the heartbreak that molded me into the standoffish woman I am today, the abandonment issues from my father that I never truly learned how to deal with, and the loss of my unborn child that has caused me to struggle with intimacy.

~

Who is the woman I look at?
Is this a selfless woman aiming for success or a puppet being controlled by other people that seem to have so much power over her?

~

How do I fully heal from the trauma I've been suppressing, and how exactly do I let it go? I haven't learned how to forgive myself. I haven't learned how to open up to my mistakes and let them go. Do I deserve to hurt?

Do I deserve to love, move on and live the life that I've been sacrificing and transitioning for? I've fallen in love before and I know those wounds will eventually heal, it just takes time; but the loss of my child has damaged me in a way that's unexplainable.

I wake up everyday remembering the feeling, the nausea and most important the 'what if' life I would've had; I let too many people get in my head. Too many people convinced me I was too young, too naive and that I would be alone. So I went against my heart and for that I hate myself.

Do I deserve to be a mother one day?
Do I deserve to love and be loved again?
Why do I feel like I hate myself so much?

I've given myself so much love, success and so many opportunities, I should be worshiping the ground that I walk on. After all this time I thought I would be healed, but it feels like new situations and experiences are throwing salt back on my wounds. I'm in pain again. I'm isolating myself again. I'm being negative again. Why do I compare myself to others that have no idea what struggles I face everyday and what its like to walk a mile in my shoes?

~

I just feel drained.

I'm exhausted from my own misunderstandings and to be honest, I wish all of my problems would just go away. Take the pressure away from my mind always thinking and figuring out shit I have no complete control over. I wish I didn't have to go through the struggle-stage because how do you remain positive during the hard times?

How do you remain content with what you have right now; if instead of what you want?
How do you bear the thought of not making it to where you wanna be?

~

Everyday I wake up with this pressure on my shoulder, to be perfect, to be great, to be influential and inspiring, but what about what I want? I want to be great, I want to be maleficent, powerful and capable of owning and changing the world. Not only for the better, but for the healthier.
But this confidence starts with me.

I'm allowing my demons to define who I am, so how do I change that? How do I block out the negativity and just live?

I'm trying the best that I can, I'm giving my all but for some odd reason society doesn't approve.

1. Why should I care about what society wants, when I'm living this life for me?
2. Why do I feel like I'm running out of time when I have so many days ahead of me?
3. Why am I so focused on the opinions of the people watching me run the race, when I'm the only one close to the finish line?

I'm tired of the pressure and the control, it's time for me to take it back and never let it go again. This moment right here I'm accepting the fact that *I need help*, I can not handle my emotions and feelings on my own; and I'm proud to say that's ok. From this moment on: I will not allow my mind to tell me who I need to be or where I should be. I'm going to brush this funk off; embrace the pain and let it guide me to my next path. My path to success and self-care. If I don't say it enough, I love you. And I will always love you.

- Tiffani Sheri Hall @*lovetiffhall_*

Notes:

Notes:

We All Tried

An Audio Tape

On the ride there,
I said my final goodbyes.
You were already gone, but I wasn't ready to let go yet.

The last few years started replaying in my head,
Like a recurring PowerPoint, a non-stop video that was in an
endless loop.
It started from the moment I met you to this moment right
now.

It was going so quickly, and I knew the car ride was only 30
minutes so.
As i looked out of the window I said to my mom, "he's gone,
isn't he?"

She looked at me and she said, "I think so".
But I knew.
You were gone way before I left to head to you, I could feel it.

We got to the hospital and everybody was already there and
they had already said their goodbyes.
I walked in the room & there you lay.

It was like you were sleeping.

I didn't want to cry because I knew this was the last time I
would ever see you again.
So I wanted to take in these final moments, even though we
weren't alone, I wanted to block everybody else out in the
room and I wanted it to just be you & I, just a few more
seconds.

So I started to talk to you.
I told you that I loved you.
& I told you that I'm sorry.

For everything that I said, I'm sorry.
I just hope that you knew I was sorry.

As I was talking to you blood started to come out of your ears
and I knew it was time to let you go.

But I wasn't ready yet. Nobody in that room was ready yet.

Your dad started to pray out loud but I just wanted everybody
to be quiet. Everybody just kept talking. But I just wanted
silence just for a few more minutes.

I wanted you to wake up.

I knew you were there. I knew you were listening. But I just
wanted you to wake up.

No matter how many times I begged you, you wouldn't wake
up.

Sooner or later I quit asking, pleading, begging God one more
chance.

I kissed your forehead, and I said goodbye.

I didn't have a choice.

You always think that you have a little bit more time, but you
never have a little bit more time you just have right now. You
just have the moment that you have right now and you have to
use it to your fullest advantage and I tried.

But I hope that you know that we all tried that night, I hope
you know.

Part 2
Therapy

To the Life I thought I would live:
With each day that passes, I am reminded that life's adventures truly shape us as individuals and emotion-baring humans. I imagined life as a child as a doctor, a lawyer, or some higher earning figure that was well-known and that you learned about in History class. But life has turned out a tad bit different and every day I am learning that that's ok.

To the Life I am Currently Living:
Everyone has a story to tell, and it doesn't make my story any worse or better than yours reading this. I hope that my stories & poems will truly reflect my life's twists & turns, fuck-ups and successes, and make yours just a tad bit easier.

I made an appointment to see a therapist,
which I was extremely excited about.
I had researched her, chose her based on her
websites' bio, & the fact she accepted my insurance,
was a big plus.
I mentally prepared for that therapist appointment
for weeks as I was very nervous and
not really sure what I should expect.
When that appointment was cancelled due to a
miscommunication, I was heartbroken.
It was scheduled at a time in my life where I (thought)
I needed her most.
And maybe that appointment would have did
some good.

~

Weeks later I started writing my journey through depression
down in an extended version of 5am Thoughts, just as I
cultivated Part 1.
With each emotion that I felt as life threw its' curveballs
at me, writing was a release I didn't know I needed.
During a time where I was looking & searching
for a safe space, a safe haven I could venture to
and find peace and solace.
It was in Part 2.
I was at a really dark place in my life when I wrote this, so this
serves as a trigger warning.
Your therapy may look a little different than mine,
in fact, I hope to frequent another one some day.
But in the meantime, I hope you read my "therapies",
and find peace and solace, too.

Enjoy.

Stories, Poems, & Journals:

<u>Part 2</u>

i have more to say, i'm still healing. *enjoy.*

"Oblivion"

"She's.. almost.. disassociated herself from the outside world. It's like, she's there, but from a distance", I saw the words written down as I was peaking in her notes.

And she was right,

I had.

"So, what exactly would you change about what happened though? In the last 2-3 years? What would you change?"

I began to answer but I hesitated.

(I don't know?)

There's a lot of shit I'd change. But there's a lot of shit I wouldn't change, either. I mean, isn't that the beauty of all of this? That life's played out exactly how it should be? Right?

"I don't know...I guess I'd go back in time and be a better friend to her. Pay more attention, I guess."

I started to itch the inner crotch of my right arm in a way that was more agitated than nervous, and I quickly wanted to finish my thought before she took it somewhere else first.

"I guess, I'd go back in time and see where things kinda went wrong. I thought I was paying attention. But I can admit, I started to get lazy. But my irritation not only stems from how I lost someone extremely close to me. It was also about the fact that everyone around me watched."

"What exactly do you mean by that?", she asked.

She sat up a little taller in her chair when she said that though..like she was, just now tuned in to what I was saying.

"Everyone who was around me was also close to me, too. Just in different ways. We all had our separate and conjoined friendships and that's just how it worked. But everyone watched. No one said anything as I was being publicly branded with an "A" on my chest, but this time in a platonic way. No one really said, 'hey guys, y'all need to sit down and work this shit out. Y'all are better than this.' That's what bothers me."

"Hmm." — she paused.

I started to itch that inner crotch again.

Journal

Have you ever considered seeing a therapist? (Y/N)

Do you think that if you have a therapist that you have a mental health issue? (Y/N)

If you had a therapist what would be the first thing you'd say when he or should would ask "What's wrong?"

"Anywhere"
July 4, 2019
3:06am

It amazes me how there was a time I was rushing to leave
this place and now it feels like I'm rushing to come back.

What was I running from, again?

I can't seem to remember.

I just remember feeling tight. Suffocated, almost, and I feel a lot like
that right now.

When that feeling creeps up I get the sudden urge to just leave & go.
Anywhere.

And that's where I want to be right now.

Anywhere.

I'm angry right now.
But I'm silent about it.
I don't care to confront.
I'm just angry right now.
Let me be.

it came in waves.
the sadness.
unpredictable & uninvited.
but it came.
i couldn't tell what the signs meant,
i just wanted to get home.
i sat there,
waiting,
others passed by going in different directions.
but here i sat,
waiting.
a wave came.
salt-water started streaming down my face &
instead of light rain this was a monsoon.
uncontrollable.
"here",
he said,
handing me a tissue.
"are you ok?"
sure.
of course i am.
"is it a boy?"
no, not this time i thought.
this time it was me.
water still raining down my face
my vision was hard to clear up.
"i just want to get home"
i thought to myself.
except,
i was almost 2000 miles away.
how do i get home?

How do I stop this?
Where do I go from here?
I'm traumatized.
From my own self,
I'm traumatized.
I feel...empty of life but full of anger.
I cannot breathe.
My chest hurts.
I'm suffocating.
I tried.
I was so full of life .. full of everything that was.
But it's almost like every time I turn around something is trying to
break my spirit.
& shit,
They won.
Shits broken.

At first,
I thought silence was the answer.
So I'd stay silent and angry.
But now,
My thoughts, it's almost as if I can feel them.
I thought being silent would kind of take that feeling away.
I didn't really know the right words to say; so silence was the clear
answer.
But my thoughts,
They hurt.
They are painful.
So many different tabs are open and I just cannot get through them
all.

Drugs help, but not so much
Nothing is working.
My thoughts seep into my dreams.
They wake me up before I'm awake and I wake up terrified.
"What's next?"
I ask myself every day.

I don't know what's coming but I pray to God it's something that will save me from whatever this is.

"Tweets"
by @T_Lloyd

"Life is not short. It is fragile.

When those words came out of my mouth six years ago, it became one of the most profound things I ever said. And maybe will say.

Since saying it and learning intimately what death looks like, I've held on to situations longer than I probably should have because I fear loss.

Death of some kind is always around the corner.

What I feel this morning, is that there are worse things than death.

Death, we can comprehend that.

But absence?

The implementation of a new norm that you didn't want or aren't ready for? I fear those too.

The adjusting. The shape shifting. The discomfort. The agony...

Certain things don't compute. Abuse, breakups, manipulation, emotional trauma. Those are heavy and most times inconceivable.

How are those manageable?

Therapy, I guess. Prayer, maybe? But also **faith & forgiveness**.

There's been a few times where I knew instantaneously that I would never be the same. That if I were to come out on the other side, I wouldn't recognize myself or the people around me.

Scary.

It's tough going to sleep with a stranger, especially when that stranger is you.

The Bible says, "Do not be afraid", but the reality is, you will be afraid.

It's ok to be scared. Do it anyway.

Move out of that state. Leave that lover. Block that toxic family member. Get that new job. Take that vacation. Restore yourself.

Search relentlessly.

Because joy is in abundance. It just might be in a place you don't frequent.

Travel for your joy. It requires it.

I'm telling you this because if you stay in the dark place, you WILL want to die. And I want you to live. I want to live.

But we have to recognize, that we will be living with a certain amount of fear.
Do it afraid.

Loss will find you. Sickness comes. Being broke happens. Most times, on a day that feels normal. It will uproot you.

Know this: live anyway.

Show up as your full self. Create enough joy so that you can lean on it during those tough times.

Do not let your trauma hold you hostage.

Because, let me tell you something, the only price trauma is willing to accept in exchange for you being free is your life.

Don't give your life away. You cannot afford it.

I've died a thousand times. I've been angry with God. I've isolated myself. I've buried myself. I saw the bad hand life dealt me and kept the cards. None of that worked in my favor.

Throw the cards back. Get up. Claw your way out. But do not make the Devil's job easier."

Is this what I get for trying to beg for intimacy when I've already given him the most intimate parts of me?
Yes?

Ok.

A long Text

"Now, I know I'm not always the easiest to deal with
& i have my crazy moments, but given these last few weeks i
think i deserve to be cut a little fucking slack.

I felt like u started to make that moment that i was trying to
enjoy with u today more difficult than it should have been.
Starting off with ur comment the other day, which we won't
discuss, it's forgotten.

But then this weekend slightly. I don't know, personally, what
expectations to have of u so i try to maintain the bare
minimum, but it's like some boundaries u cross unintentionally.
and idk if that's because i haven't been vocal or I'm not sure.

But even in last minute moments when i decide to come to
come see you out of town it's like very little consideration from
u is shown. Like i said, idk if it is intentional or unintentional
or what.

Consideration to me, looks like at least some time should be sat
aside for us to do something productive & engaging.

But when u come back to the room, we fuck, u leave. Then u
come back, u sleep. We wake up, we fuck, u leave. U come
back, you pack your stuff, u give me a kiss then leave .. like do
u see where one person would be feeling quite ... empty after
those said interactions?

Essssssspecially after everything that has happened u think
that i would wanna feel like ... Whatever."

some shit is just unforgivable.

"House Party"

I stood there, trying to balance myself with the ball in front of me and my club, trying to aim perfectly.

To be perfectly honest, I have no idea how to "shoot" this thing or hit it or whatever you're supposed to do.

My form wasn't that good, either. I look so stupid, ugh. Hopefully he doesn't notice.

"Whew!", shouted my friend in the background as he saw the ball fling barely into the air.

"I think that went well", I said hoping someone would agree with me.

I have on my glasses and you would think I could see 20/20 but, I can't. I feel like it's even harder to see clearly with these damn glasses on some times.

I'm alert, though.

Making sure I pay attention if he walks inside or he just happens to walk up where me and a bunch of his friends are standing casually shooting golf balls in an empty field.

Yea, so. He's never given me the 'knight in shining armor' kinda vibes even though I kind-of thrusted them upon him so why would he start now?

Yikes.

Untitled

It seems as if disappointment is inevitable.
It's always around the corner somehow, lurking.
Fishing for its' next victim.
Who am I kidding?
I'm not alone here. Not in this.

It was fear.
Fear makes you do stupid things.

My fear caused me to ignore.
Boy, do I regret that.

Oblivion cont'd.

"Talk to me ..about him", she said nervously. I assume it was because she was fearful of my response.

I took my right index finger and wrapped it around my left index finger and began to rub it like I was jacking it off.

I looked at her, and then I looked away.

"What about him?"

"Well, if you could say anything to him, right now, what would you say?"

I started rubbing my finger again, a little rougher this time.

I looked back at her,

"I hope he has a good life."

She didn't look surprised that I said that. Like she was almost expecting it. I didn't know what more to say. I froze almost, but I'm not sure. It was odd.

"Ok. Well, if you could say anything to him right now, and he's not here, what would you say?"

"You could talk directly to me", she affirmed.

On the wall to the left of her was a John Mayer poster I couldn't keep my eyes off of. I didn't know if it was because I thought John Mayer was absolutely stunning, or because 'Slow Dancing In A Burning Room' makes me cry every time I hear it, and it I started to hear it play faintly in the back of my head.

Great.

I gave her eye contact and started to rub my finger more gentler,

"I would say.."

She nodded at me.

"I would think that I would tell him I was pissed but, that's not entirely true, I think my feelings are hurt more than I was pissed."

She looked impressed.

"I get it, ya know, that the people you care about or even love at times will hurt you. That it doesn't make them exempt from hurting or even disappointing you, I get that. I understand that, y'know?

But you show up for each other. I don't think you have to be in a committed relationship to do that. And I know we weren't in one, I get that, truly I do. That was never going to happen."

"What do you mean?", She interrupted me.

"I knew we were never going to be together in the way I would have ever wanted us to. So in a way at times I altered what I wanted. To accommodate me? I'd like to think so. But I know it was more-so to accommodate him.

When I met him in the club; the first night I ever saw him he was sitting in the back, slumped over just a tad, not drawing any attention to himself, but beautiful. I thought he was the most beautiful man I had ever seen. I was with my friends at the time and we were walking towards where he was sitting so I stopped the group mid-track and told them I was going to marry him.

Creepy vibes, yeah I know, I said that too. But he was so beautiful and handsome and I immediately wanted a family. I had never felt that way before. Even in the relationship I was in for almost 2 years I struggled with the idea of seeing a family with him. But here I am, seeing him for the first time, this beautiful man, & I want to have his babies. Particularly a son! That's all I really want. But anyway, I knew that was impossible."

"Well, why it would be impossible?", she asked.

"Why would he want me? Look at me. I'm 24. He's grown, established, he has a family. Him and his child's mother they have a schedule on how they manage their kids, why would he want to include me in that? He probably looks at me as some kid when I have worked so hard to define my own femininity and womanhood. I didn't see a light at the end of that tunnel, so I settled."

"How did you settle?"

"Because I could never have him in the way that I wanted him so I settled for the only way he could have me."

"Um hm.."

"Listen, and this isn't to say that I wanted a relationship with him. I don't know what I want with him. I don't even really think I knew him!

I don't really think he knows me either, tbh.

We've almost spent the last year talking to each other every day & seeing each other every few weeks or so, except it's been very recent in the last few weeks. But, I don't really know him. I think that's what hurts me the most.

But, I don't really have anyone else to blame. I try to blame him and I can, but only for his actions. Not for my after or before thoughts when I knew, this would not end well for me. This man is someone who I have literally not gone a day without speaking to in months, and he barely knows me either.

What I know now, is that the one time I asked him to show up for me, he didn't. I don't think I could ever forgive him for that."

"Why do you think that you can't forgive him? Remember you said tha.."

"Yes, I remember what I said", interrupting her.

"I get that even the people you love and care about can and will hurt you too."

"So why do you think you can't forgive him?" She said confused.

I started rubbing my finger again.

A melody

Sometimes when we feel sad
we take our own lives and then we feel bad.
We wake up and try to live for each day,
And I'll try and I'll try to forgive you anyway.

When moments pass & I feel blue,
I try to remind myself about the good in you.
I envision the memories like dreams they appear,
but they fade so quickly like they were never there.

Oh, tell me what you needed.
I thought I had done all I could to make sure we succeed.
Oh, tell me what I can do.
Tell me how can I make myself stop loving you.

Acceptance

I'll never know that man.
The man that sweeps you off your feet,
& tells you you're the most beautiful woman he's ever laid eyes
on.
I'll never know that man.

I've come to terms and acceptance that the man I knew and the
man you will show to the woman you love will be different.

Why do you keep trying to hold onto me when you know you
cannot love me the way I need to be loved?
It's so selfish of you.
Having me repeat the same things just so you can have a few
moments to gather your excuses.
You know what I'm talking about.
For months I wish I would know that man.
You are so beautiful to me. But you make me feel so ugly
inside.

I don't want to know you any more.

I'm afraid that my thoughts are an illusion.
I'm afraid that I've created an idea of who this man is in my head and he is not it.
I'm afraid that if I express my wants and needs that they won't be met.
I'm afraid of me, of who I've been, of who I'm supposed to be.
I don't recognize myself.
I can't even look myself in the mirror.
I can't do my hair. Brush my teeth. Wash my face.
I don't know who I am anymore.
But what I'm afraid of most is finding that out.
This woman who I've been I don't understand her.
Why would she wait until her body shuts down?
I touch the scars above my ovaries and I'm taken back to that place again.
That place was an immense amount of loneliness.
I feel pain.
Large amounts of pain.
I just want to quiet the voices.
But I'm afraid of my medicine. I'm afraid it might kill me.
I don't know where to go anymore.
I'm afraid home won't recognize me.

I laughed a lot today and that felt good.

I remember when my debt would wake me up out of my sleep. I would wake up at 7am gasping for air because the amount would haunt me.

My fear was infiltrating my dreams.

I was away on a bachelorette trip in Las Vegas and I woke up the next morning again around 7am after falling asleep shortly after 4 unable to sleep. Unable to really dream without that thought in the back of my head.

I would wake up and immediately check my email. Preparing myself for a reminder that I never got. I wonder when that's gonna come back. I know it can't be gone forever. But I wonder when.

"That Dick Doesn't Love You" 4:23am

Are you addicted to the pain?
To the slight emotional abuse?
Are you addicted to the vicious cycle of unrequited love?
What type of love do you think you deserve?

What is the true difference between them?
It's like, you accepted the same lack of consideration and emotional
unavailability from them both, but you easily cut him off. But why
not *him*?

What was the difference?

He did something that was disrespectful and you cut him off with no
hesitation.

But *he* did things that were disrespectful for months but you tolerate
it from him?

Why is that?

What is it about him that you are willing to lose bits and pieces of
your self integrity?

Is it the dick?

That dick doesn't love you.
That dick doesn't care about you.
That dick doesn't consider you.
That dick gave you a baby and didn't want it.
That dick could give a damn about you.

So why do you want that dick so bad, when you can have a dick that
loves you back?

Journal

What about the dick you're currently sucking. Ask yourself, "Does that dick love me?"

That dick doesn't

_____

That dick doesn't

_____

That dick doesn't

_____

That dick doesn't

_____

That dick doesn't

_____

That dick does

_____

That dick does

_____

That dick does

_____

That dick does

_____

That dick does

_____

Prayer

Dear God,
I've been trying to figure out where the direction of my life is
headed and I don't know why I didn't think to ask you directly.
In the midst of my darkness it didn't even cross my mind.
It's like, you were the last person I thought to reach out to.
Humans fail because we are not perfect but you are and I
knew that, but I seemed to have forgot it.
When I was crying out the other day, yelling in anger and
dissatisfaction, you were there and I didn't consider you.
I don't think it was intentional.
I wanted to die.
I couldn't see the light.
I couldn't see the protection, or forgiveness, or grace you have
given me countless of times before.
All I saw was darkness.
All I felt was darkness.
Today I cry out to you in pain.
I know you feel it more than I ever could bare.
But I don't want to be in pain anymore.
What do I need to do to pull myself out of this dark place?

After I talk to God I feel better.

I was angry at myself for being depressed all those months and not looking for a job.

I was angry at myself because I was scared to get a new job and fail at it.

I was angry at myself for asking that man to let me ride with him on his boat.

I was angry at myself for disappointing people.

I was angry at myself for not being able to show up for my friends.

I was angry at myself for my bad financial habits.

I was angry at myself for trying to make you care about me.

I was angry at myself because you didn't care about me like I wanted you to.

I was angry at myself for not cutting you off when I should have, then I probably wouldn't be this angry at myself.

I was angry at myself for ignoring the signs that my body was trying to show me, maybe I wouldn't have lost my unborn child.

I was angry at myself for being afraid.

I was angry at myself for not speaking up for myself.

I was angry at myself for not asking for help when I knew I needed it.

I was angry at myself for not eating.

I was angry at myself for losing weight.

I was angry at myself for not taking care of my mind.

I can play the blame game all day and point the finger at other people but that does nothing for me. My disappointment within myself sent me into a depression that I didn't think I would make it out of. I turned to some friends and family and felt alone. I was alone, and I was angry about it.

Journal

We all have those moments where disappointment and even anger tend to take over our lives. In my journey to forgiveness and recovery, I've found it therapeutic to write out my 'angers'. You should too:

I'm angry at myself for

_____

I'm angry at myself for

_____

I'm angry at myself for

_____

I'm angry at myself for

_____

I'm angry at myself for

_____

I'm angry at myself for

_____

I'm angry at myself for

_____

I'm angry at myself for

_____

I'm angry at myself for

_____

I'm angry at myself for

_____

Oblivion cont'd.

"It wasn't his fault..not necessarily", I said.

She looked puzzled.

"What I mean by that is, he's been the exact same person since I knew him. He hasn't changed. He's always been emotionally disconnected and very short and concise. I hated it 6 months ago just as I do now. So he hasn't changed. I changed, I guess, and even that was unintentional."

"Now, when you say that he hasn't changed, do you mean that because he's always been the same person or that your expectations of him changed and that's why you can't forgive him?", she asked.

"Yes & No.", I answered.

"I wanted him to be this person to me. Not a husband, but a little more than a friend. I thought I had done a good job asking for that. But, maybe I didn't."

"So why can't you forgive him?", she said looking puzzled again.

"Because, what is there really to forgive? He doesn't even know fully what I'm asking for and I've explained it and given him plenty of examples and he doesn't want to get it. He can't give me what I'm asking for. I know he cares about me, but not in the way I want him to. So, it isn't necessary to forgive him, but I do think it is necessary to forgive myself."

"Bingo."

She wasn't puzzled anymore.

"That's what I wanted you to say. Forgive him for what? He's not sorry. He doesn't think he did anything wrong. According to him, you both made an agreement based on the dynamic of the relationship that you both asked for, and he abided by those terms. What you were looking for? He can't give you. You knew that then & you knew that now. Only difference between then and now is a baby was in the mix, and you both got in your feelings."

"He still selfishly kept me around", I rebutted.

"He knew he couldn't give me what I was asking for and he didn't say that. I wasn't asking for commitment. I wasn't asking for his hand in marriage. Only thing I wanted was to be considered & more of an emotional connection".

"But, why would you even want to ask for that?", she replied.

I started rubbing my finger again.

My Journey to Self-Forgiveness

It took me a while to apologize to my past-self for accepting and tolerating behavior and settling for things I should have never let step foot into my life. I still find myself apologizing for it daily. At times I find myself getting angry; yelling out to the sky, screaming into my pillow, taking naps to sleep away the disappointment. But it creeps up on me at the most inconvenient times. What's worse are the reminders. The reminders from my parents, other people, friends, etc; I'm already constantly reminding myself. That voice is already, always, in the back of my head. It's even harder being on social media at times watching others live the life that I know I deserve I should live. Traveling from country to country, vacationing on yachts, trying new foods. Here I am, stuck at an unfamiliar place, barely eating because I'm sad.

In my current journey I find myself most times more confused than intentional. At the beginning of 2019 to be "Intentional" was my mantra. I wanted to enter and leave things with the intent to keep them there or make them go away, as needed. I set goals for myself to achieve each month so that by the end of the year, I would look back and see all of the progress I had made. I guess it was after month 3 that I started to realize the initial idea and intent I had for my life had changed. But, I've recently realized that there is truly **beauty in the struggle**. Even though I'm not necessarily on the other side of my struggle just yet, the light at the end of this tunnel seems to get brighter with each day that passes. Living a healthy lifestyle can contribute to this mindset. What's healthy for me may not be healthy for you. But I find myself really enjoying my alone time but also realizing that I have to be out amidst other people as well.

Sometimes I get so comfortable alone, that I'll look up and it's been weeks since I've had any healthy human interaction. I also realized how unhealthy that is. Being alone and feeling alone isn't the goal, at least not for me. But in my journey to self-forgiveness, I've also found that in order to not repeat unhealthy behavior, I have to admit that I don't like it. Sometimes after falling in the trap of a routine for so long, and that routine could be the feeling of disappointment, after a while you may even start to *enjoy* that feeling. I hated my struggle so much that at times I started to enjoy it. It's a sick mindset but I've learned totally natural.

<u>Forgiveness looks like grace</u>. The grace you ask other people to give you, you have to give to yourself.

You have to say to yourself:

"Self,
I'm sorry, that wasn't kind of me.
I'll do better next time."

Drink more water. Go out to more happy hours. Light that blunt. Just always have the intent to do better next time.

A Short Story

I was driving up and down the coast,
looking for the perfect spot to watch the sunset.
I pulled over into this pier,
there were small boats docked and large rocks I
could sit on to ensure the perfect view.
I saw a man docking his ship and I mustered up the
courage to ask "Can I have a ride?"
How silly of me.
I've traveled all around the world by myself and with
strangers,
and I usually always think twice.
This time I let my guard down just a little too low.
He of course agreed, but spoke very little English.
He seemed like a harmless old man.
Not young but not 70.
We rode out into the sunset,
waves crashing, the boat handling whatever came it's way on
its own, and we stopped.
I grew excited as I wanted to take a dip in the ocean for just a
bit.
The sun was going down so I know we needed to head back
soon, but I just wanted 5 more minutes.
I got back on the boat, drenched and without a towel. I sat out
to sunbathe as he drove back to shore.
He paused & asked for a sexual favor.
I said no thanks, let's go back.
I was confused & the moment he asked I said "my dumb ass",
I'm in the Caribbean where things and mentalities are just a
tad bit different.
I'm 24 but I get mistaken for 16 1/2 daily, I wonder how old he
thought I was.
He asked again, grabbing my arm to pull me closer, again, I
said "No thanks, take me back".

He said no,
I had to do this.

It was getting dark and we were a few miles away from shore
and I started to get a little scared.
I know he couldn't speak much English but "No" is universal,
right?
We get in a slight tussle and at this point, I'm shaking.
I just wanted a boat ride.

Oblivion cont'd.

"You know what I realized?"

She sat up straight in her chair, intrigued.

"It took me a while to get over that break up. At times I don't think I'm really over it. I still miss her sometimes, ya know? I think I just recently realized that I was broken up with. That sucks, ya know? How do you really move on from that?"

"I think you are moving on from it, it just doesn't look as glamorous as you thought it would."

"Life is shitty", I said under my breath.

"Is that really it though? 15 years of friendship, just thrown away. I was so caught off guard ..."

She interrupted me,

"Let that go."

She was right.

How do I fit in?

I had been dreading coming home for a while.
I had moved away from here 6 years ago,
and have since only visited days at a time.
But since I moved back to kind of sort out my life,
I notice how everyone here has a life of their own &
I don't kinda fit in.
It makes me sad.
I know my solitude may come off intentional,
but I've been alone for so long it's like I've forgotten basic
human interaction.
It makes me uncomfortable at times.
Sometimes I'm unsure of what to say,
how to keep the conversation going ya know?
Idk I get so wrapped up in the semantics sometimes I just lose
sight of the real shit.
My mom invited me out the house tonight to an event and I
should have went.
I thought about the process of doing my hair and make up and
instantly got turned off.
I thought about the smile I would have to keep on my face at
the Country club and opted for a sub and beer at the house.
My sister got home from work shortly after my mom got back,
and my dad is preparing for a major event he's putting on
tomorrow.
Everyone is out living their lives,
going to work,
conversing with friends,
and then there's me.
How do I fit in?

What do you do
when you realize you are homesick,
but you don't recognize home anymore?

Where do you go?

I feel numb. I don't feel anything.

Dear my depression,

You've isolated me from friends & you've isolated me from myself.
I spend days trying to figure out how to fight you. Trying to figure out how to not let you win.

Can we ever go back to who we've been?
You know, as people we evolve and we become new versions of ourselves; we develop new habits, but can we ever go back to who we've been if we don't like who we've become?
Maybe it's because we've actually always been this way? I'm not really sure.

I moved out of my house when I was 18 years old to go to college 20 minutes away.
I very rarely ever came home and I know my mom believes it's because I didn't like home, or her;
But that's not the truth.

I'm not really sure why I didn't come home that often. In my mind I believed I did.
There were times where me and my friends would come over for dinner, or I'd come home on a Sunday and wash clothes before we would have family dinner.
That was even when I had got my first apartment.

I didn't really come home that often junior & senior year mainly because I was studying abroad and other things that required more attention than I actually could give it.
But I still gave it though.
Nobody really saw me that often, not even my roommates.
It was a stressful time period in my life. It was the "what's the first job after college" conversation every 5 minutes and I wasn't the biggest fan.

After college, I feel like I isolated my own-self.
It wasn't intentional at first.

I had just entered a new relationship and we did everything
together.
(you know how that goes)
But we were in love, our own version of it, and it worked for a
while.
But about 8 months it didn't work as well as I thought it
would.

I was struggling with my own personal insecurities.
I felt I was struggling with making friends and maintaining the
current friendships I had.
I didn't really enjoy going out, but in college I enjoyed going
out often so that was an odd transition for me.
The times where I made myself go out and try and be social I
found that hard to do.
I found it hard to maintain conversations and interests, and I
was entering a state of depression that has lasted over a year.
I was not prepared for that.

Our break-up incited a series of unfortunate events.
All had nothing to do with him and more of me.
I found myself in a very dark place.
At times, I ask myself was that break-up needed to pivot me
into the direction where I'm going now?

I wonder.

I keep fighting you.
I haven't always been this way.
But the battle is becoming more than I can bare.
I write to get it all out.
But reading the words is painful.
I feel like I'm drowning.
Like I can't keep my head above water.
One happy moment is followed by darkness.
I don't know when the next wave will hit.
I'm afraid.
Afraid of what I might do to quiet the voices.
So I put my head under my covers,
and I cry it away,
hoping that I'll feel better afterwards.
But this time I don't.
I find myself asking is this real?
No way this is my life.
When did I become like this?
What *made* me like this?
I just want it to stop.
I want it to go away & never come back.
I want depression to be foreign to me.
I want to see it & not recognize it.
I want to go back to the way I was.
But I can't feel anything.
I can't feel.
I tell myself to breathe in & out,
that this moment doesn't last forever.
But I'm afraid that it does.
I'm afraid that it does last forever.
I can't remember the good times,
but they happened right? They had to.
All I see is darkness.
All I feel is sadness.
I don't want to die, but I don't want to live either.

Oblivion cont'd.

"I need you to talk to me, about that day, that experience. I imagine it was heavy?", she said.

"It was", I answered looking at that John Mayer poster behind her, rubbing my finger again.

I knew this was something I needed to talk about but I wasn't quite sure the words I should use.

"I was cold. Then I was hot. The pain was unbearable, and I was lonely. Oh my god I was so lonely. I had never felt that lonely in my life. Actually, yes I have. There was a time I was living in Milan and I didn't leave my apartment for at least 10 days. It reminded me a lot like that feeling. It could've killed me."

"The loneliness or the pain?", she asked.

"Both." I said.

"Both could've killed me. My mother was a few hundred miles away, he was too. My friends were nowhere to be found, except the ones who made it a point to tell me they were there. That made me feel a little bit warmer. But I was surrounded by doctors running tests. They were trying to figure out what was wrong with me and I didn't know either I just felt an immense amount of pain.

And then boom. It burst.

My Fallopian tube had burst and I lost the baby."

"That must have terrible. I'm so sorry you had to go through that.", she said.

"Yeah, it was ass I'm not gonna lie. The worst pain I have ever felt in my life to this date. I've been in a few car accidents, broken both arms at the same time, had my heart broken over the last few years too, but that pain, that pain was a different type of pain. I wouldn't wish it on my worst enemy.

I tried to be strong though. But when the doctor told me she had to remove one of my tubes I just started crying. I didn't even know what that really meant. Could I have a baby again? I mean, I wasn't trying this time but in the future I want to have a baby, I think. Any-who, I started to become really afraid when they said I needed to go into emergency surgery. No one familiar was around me and I felt sick to my stomach, literally."

"How was your recovery?"

"I wanted to kill my self."

She wasn't that shocked I said that, but concerned nonetheless.

"What happened?", she asked.

"I felt even lonelier. The percs they prescribed lasted maybe two days for a recovery that was expected to be 4-6 weeks. Dumb as shit. They gave me a total of 12. 2 I was supposed to take every 8-12 hours or so. So you could see how they were gone pretty quickly. The first day after my recovery I wasn't able to do anything. I actually underestimated what recovery actually looked like. I thought I would be mobile and even tried to attend one of my best friend's' birthday brunch but I could barely get out of bed. Walking was non-existent. It's as if I had completely lost my balance. My appetite was shit. And no one was there but me."

I had moments of extreme sadness & then moments of extreme anger. I tried to smoke the depression away, that didn't work, but it helped. Thinking back to those moments, honestly scares

207

me. It embarrasses me really. Some of the people who I thought would show up for me, didn't. It taught me a valuable lesson."

"I noticed that you have a hard time asking for help. Is that something you are looking to improve? Because everyone needs help..I hope you know you aren't alone in this.", she gently reminded me.

"Yes, it's embarrassing. I was in a depressive episode once and I texted my mom letting her know I was having a hard time. It took me 30 minutes to send that text because I was going back and forth with myself about what her reaction might be. I knew she would immediately call me and want to talk things out, but I didn't really want to do that. But I also knew it was what I needed."

"And how did you feel after you talked things out with your mother?", she asked.

"I guess a little better. I still struggled with it though because I don't think she quite understood what I was telling her. Just because she see's me laughing and even smiling sometimes, there are a lot of unhappy moments that she doesn't see, and that's of course because I don't want her or anybody else to see them. Being in that depressive state, feeling numb, crying, my room full of darkness..is not an easy thing to witness nor to explain to someone else. The fact that I'm even talking about it right now, is shocking to me."

"I think that's good, though. The fact that you are talking about it right now, here in this moment. Do you feel a little bit better at least?", she asked

"I do. I just, I don't know."

"You just what?"
"I just want all of this shit to go away."

This book saved my life
The End

A Playlist

To anyone who ever broke my heart, these songs help me feel better.

https://music.apple.com/us/playlist/feel-better-songs/pl.u-NpXm9LgTpLgPaB

Alive - Kehlani
Almost is Never Enough - Ariana Grande
Belief (Stripped Version) - Gavin DeGraw
Beyond - Leon Bridges
Blessed - Daniel Caesar
Breakeven - The Script
Change - TEEKS
Daughters - John Mayer
Death & Taxes - Daniel Caesar
Do Me Baby - Ball Greezy
DYWM - Nao
Finally - James Arthur
Finest Hour - Gavin DeGraw
Finish Line - Chance the Rapper, Kirk Franklin, Noname, T-Pain
Fly Before You Fall - Cynthia Ervin
Follow Through - Gavin DeGraw
For The First Time - The Script
Godspeed - Frank Ocean
Good Thing - Sam Smith
Heartbreak Warfare - John Mayer
Hold You In My Arms - Ray LaMontagne
Hopelessly Devoted - Play
I Didn't Mean To Fall In Love - Snoh Aalegra
I Don't Want To - Alessia Cara
I Would - Justin Bieber
If Only - TEEKS
I'm Gonna Find Another You - John Mayer
I'm Not The Only One - Sam Smith
I Think You've Got You Fools Mixed Up - Brenton Wood
Japanese Denim - Daniel Caesar
Landslide - Fleetwood Mac
Let It Be Me - Ray LaMontagne
Little Rowboat - Daniel Caesar
Loved By You - KIRBY
Love Like That - Snoh Aelgra
Make It Out Alive (*feat. SiR*) - Nao
Meaning - Gavin DeGraw
Mirror - Madison Ryann Ward
Mountains to Move - Gavin DeGraw
My Love Is Like A Star - Demi Lovato
(Nice To Meet You) Anyway - Gavin DeGraw
Never Be Apart - TEEKS
Nikes - Frank Ocean

Nothing - The Script
Oh, How it Hurts - Barbara Mason
One Less Lonely Girl - Justin Bieber
Only Wanna Be With You - Samm Henshaw
On the Wings of Love - Jeffrey Osborne
Orbit - Nao
Over-Rated - Gavin DeGraw
Please Don't Stop The Rain - James Morrison
Precious Love - James Morrison
Reality - Allen Stone
River - Leon Bridges
Run Every Time - Gavin DeGraw
Same Drugs - Chance the Rapper
Sandcastles - Beyoncé
Saturn *(feat. Kwabs)* - Nao
Self Control - Frank Ocean
Siegfried - Frank Ocean
She Is Love - Parachute
Shelter - Ray LaMontagne
Show No Regret - Daniel Caesar
Slow Dancing In A Burning Room - John Mayer
Soldier - Gavin DeGraw
Solo - Frank Ocean
Speechless - Dan + Shay
Spell It Out - Gavin DeGraw
Streetcar - Daniel Caesar
Still In Love *(feat. Eryn Allen Kane)* - Thirdstory
Sunday Candy - Chance the Rapper
SUPERSTITION *(feat. John Mayer)* - Daniel Caesar
Take It All - Kiana Ledé
Take It All - Adele
Take Me Away *(feat. Syd)* - Daniel Caesar
The Key - Madison Ryann Ward
Thinking Of You - Katy Perry
Transform *(feat. Charlotte Day Wilson)* - Daniel Caesar
Two Worlds Collide - Demi Lovato
U Smile - Justin Bieber
Understand - Shawn Mendes
Use My Shoulder - Jojo
Wanna Be Happy? - Kirk Franklin
War Baby - Roddy Rich
Wash Over Me - TEEKS
We Find Love - Daniel Caesar
Where You're At - Allen Stone
Who Hurt You? - Daniel Caesar
Yellow Of The Sun - Nao